CHILE

Also by Jacobo Timerman

Prisoner Without a Name, Cell Without a Number

The Longest War: Israel in Lebanon

CHILE
Death in the South

Jacobo Timerman

Translated from the Spanish by
Robert Cox

VINTAGE BOOKS

A Division of Random House
New York

FIRST VINTAGE BOOKS EDITION, OCTOBER 1988

Translation copyright © 1987 by Alfred A. Knopf, Inc.

All rights reserved under International and Pan-American Copyright
Conventions. Published in the United States by Random House, Inc.,
New York, and simultaneously in Canada by Random House of Canada
Limited, Toronto. Originally published, in hardcover, by Alfred A. Knopf,
Inc., a division of Random House, Inc., New York, in 1987. Translated
from an unpublished Spanish-language manuscript by Jacobo Timerman.
Copyright by Jacobo Timerman.

Library of Congress Cataloging-in-Publication Data
Timerman, Jacobo, 1923–
Chile: death in the south.
1. Chile—Politics and government—1973–
2. Pinochet Ugarte, Augusto. 3. Human rights—Chile—
History—20th century. 4. Violence—Chile—History—
20th century. I. Title.
[F3100.T54 1988]   983'.0647   88-40029
ISBN 0-679-72012-x (pbk.)

MANUFACTURED IN THE UNITED STATES OF AMERICA
10 9 8 7 6 5 4 3 2 1

FOR STANLEY K. SHEINBAUM

A CONCERNED AMERICAN

DEAD GALLOP

Like ashes, like seas peopling themselves,
in the submerged slowness, in the shapelessness . . .
                                                                Pablo Neruda

(From *Residence on Earth*, translated by Donald Walsh,
                                        New Perspectives, 1973)

CHILE

1

Every moment of the day, Chileans speak incessantly of Chile. Although their hearts burst with anguish, anxiety, and nostalgia, they never stop speaking of Chile. Throughout the long blue nights in their cities, they speak of Chile. It is surprising how intensely Chileans feel that Chile is Chile. They know it represents fear and trembling, but they believe in the magic of the name. They feel they are proprietors of this name, Chile. And this possession strengthens them more than any ideology.

Years of dictatorship by the last Prussian army in the world have not separated Chileans from Chile. The military rulers have prevented them from living like human beings, but they have not been able to prevent them from surviving like Chileans.

Chileans say that life goes on in the churches, the courtrooms, and the cemeteries. The rest is survival. They will survive General Pinochet and the dictatorship, because on the other side of their bondage is Chile.

They take refuge in the churches, seeking consolation or the strength to extend the space in which they can fight the regime. They go from courtroom to courtroom with volunteer—almost suicidal—lawyers to defend their relatives, to search for the missing, and to get the condemned released from the prisons. They also visit the cemeteries so that the graves of those murdered by the military will remind them not to forget.

But they do all this like sleepwalkers, as if they are in too much of a state of shock to realize the risks they are taking.

A mother tells her twelve-year-old son: "Don't ask questions, don't get involved in anything. When you go to college, Pinochet will no longer be here."

The poet Pablo Neruda had a vision of this Chilean necessity to survive, of this Chilean attachment to life, when he wrote in his *Ceremonial Songs:*

> *We don't go, nor return, nor know.*
> *With our eyes closed, we exist.*

It is the great strength of the oppressed and humiliated: to exist. It is the "We Shall Overcome" of Martin Luther King, Jr. In the streets of Chile, with Hispanic rhetoric, the tough, tender, and sober conviction of Alabama.

The general commanded a parachute regiment when he was named rector of the University of Chile. In full uniform, with boots well polished, he dropped by parachute into the gardens of the university.

This caused no undue surprise. The entire country was occupied, and each general chose his own way of conquering the territory assigned to him. All the generals and admirals had dreamed of a war in which victory would allow them to take control of the cities of Bolivia, Peru, or Argentina, and so the occupation of Chile gave free rein to their fantasies, awakening such obsessions and desires as were thought to have been buried with Hitler in Berlin in 1945. Combine this neurosis with impunity, and you have a picture of a boorish military man—neurotic yet invulnerable, overconfident through ignorance and programmed by his cowardice—assuming total power over universities, prisons, factories, villages, cities, libraries, kindergartens, supermarkets, publishing houses, newspapers, studios, and theaters.

The general stepped out of his parachute, handed it to one of his young aides, and ordered university administrators to initiate legal proceedings against all the professors. The investigations were so detailed that they delved into the political, moral, family, and scientific backgrounds of every member of the faculty.

Some professors were arrested on the spot. Others went underground or into exile. Those who remained, with some of the deans who were not purged, engaged in a minimum of resistance. They refused to institute investigations without formal charges or to act on anonymous accusations. In this way they managed to reduce the number of charges brought against faculty members. Later they dared a little more, allowing those accused the chance to defend themselves. After they had secured this right of defense, expulsion could be effected only at the conclusion of a long legal process.

The university administrators managed to retain most of the teaching staff, but not the quality or content of the teaching.

The professors and deans decided to go further. They organized a "shadow cabinet" to plan studies, to maintain contacts with the outside world, to teach the expelled students surreptitiously, and to replace with private funds the scholarships that were annulled by the military.

Many of them, however, became demoralized and fell into deep depression. Although, in the School of Engineering, they kept a photograph of J. Robert Oppenheimer on the wall, they felt like German scientists awaiting the death of Hitler.

They were—and still are—rational and cautious. Their caution has kept them alive and in Chile. But their rationality has had its limits: the stupidity of the Chilean military.

They thought, perhaps, that they might establish a dialogue with the military by appealing to their patriotism. But they discovered how difficult it is for a military man who feels omnipotent in occupied enemy territory to harbor any patriotic sentiments toward this territory. For the Chilean military, Chile was occupied territory.

The professors wrote studies and drew up a program for restructuring the Chilean economy. They planned a leap into the future for an economy that was tied tightly to the fluctuations of the price of copper on international markets. They not only revamped the production methods in the copper mines, to forestall exhaustion, they also planned a program to develop the economy by exporting timber and lithium, products that have never been systematically exploited. They also proposed to reorganize agriculture and introduce new products.

The Chilean military refused to consider studies by scientists who, however timidly, had ever protested violations of human rights.

Contemplating that photograph of Oppenheimer, a scientist explained his predicament: "Don't ask me not to question and also expect me to think. If I think, I cannot be unquestioning."

Some think; others are unquestioning. Some are in jail, some have been murdered, many are in exile. And more, many more, the length and breadth of this long, narrow, cold country, remain cocooned in a tranquil cynicism, awaiting the death of Hitler.

They wanted to be pragmatists, but they turned into opportunists. They wanted to maintain academic values, scientific rationality, but they did not struggle and resist. With enormous energy and enthusiasm, they turned to nostalgia. They fortified themselves spiritually and strengthened themselves by remembering what Chile used to be. Nostalgia became the great justification. It was like a promise that everything would again be as it once was if only one preserved one's existence.

One of these scientists, in a dusty, almost dirty office at the University of Chile, sought consolation in a moral lamentation because he could not find an explanation in his privileged and organized mind: "What changed in Chile? We have lost the capacity to feel the suffering of our neighbor as if it were our own. We are not moved by the suffering of another person. Perhaps not even moved by our own suffering. Chileans no longer feel anything."

On his desk was a sheet of white paper covered with thick writing in red ink—you can find it in any of the little theaters and bars of Bellavista, Santiago's bohemian quarter. It is a poem by Mikhail Lermontov, the nineteenth-century Russian poet:

> *Land of scoundrels, farewell!*
> *Land of masters, land of slaves!*
> *You, in your neat blue uniforms,*
> *You who live only to obey, like slaves.*
> *In my exile, if only I could find*
> *peace under Caucasian skies,*
> *far from defamers and the czars,*
> *far from constantly spying eyes.*

Sigmund Freud and Karl Marx have had little luck with Latin American dictatorships. Their books have been burned, at worst, or they have been banned. Study of their work in universities was prohibited, because they were held to blame for the misfortunes that some interludes of democracy have unleashed in Latin America. There were dictatorships that have also denounced—although not publicly—Albert Einstein and even Pope John XXIII, the latter for introducing democratic ideas and methods into the Catholic Church.

Only the Chilean military, however, could have come to the conclusion that Friedrich Nietzsche posed a danger to the future of Chile. In Nietzsche's nihilism they discovered an obstacle to the organized society that General Augusto Pinochet was constructing for Chile. Nietzsche was seen as a threat to the return to what Pinochet, in moments of generosity, calls "full democracy." When speaking as a strategist, he makes reference to "protected democracy." When he is in a paternal mood, he talks of "democracy that is worth living." Finally, there is "fortified democracy." That is his term of choice when he is explaining to the military officer corps why he, Augusto Pinochet, must in 1989 succeed Augusto Pinochet.

In the home of one of Pinochet's ex-ministers you are likely to see your host in a photograph of a Pinochet cabinet. In the picture, Pinochet himself is seated in the center of the front row, in a chair higher than the others. Behind him is a row of people who are standing. The majority are military officers, in dress uniform. The civilian men wear tailcoats, the lone woman a long dress. The room is huge, a palace salon. The expressions on the faces of Chile's masters are calm, satisfied—even good-humored.

The Chileans regarded their cultured and well-ordered country, once the most stable democracy in Latin America, as a European nation. To them, Chile was "the England of the South." In 1973 they discovered, and have continued discovering every day since, that they cannot escape their savage Latin American destiny.

It is not the British Empire, even at its most splendid, that the imperial photograph recalls. Some of Pinochet's ex-ministers confide that they felt they were at the court of a Russian czar.

The military regime—which includes in its power structure the army, navy, air force, and carabineros (the national police force)—that emerged in September 1973 with the death of Salvador Allende was converted first into an army regime and then into a government dominated by Pinochet himself. He wasn't left in charge—he imposed himself as dictator. His only problem has been the discovery that maintaining absolute power is much more difficult than achieving it. In his first thirteen years not only did a new generation of civilians come to the fore, so did a new military generation.

Those psychologists who have remained in Chile find in Pinochet's thoroughgoing understanding of military life the key to his ability to create an image of himself as a powerful and unchallenged emperor. He manipulates the armed forces as if he were one of the gods of antiquity, rewarding or punishing, granting favors and demanding loyalty.

Pinochet has succeeded in converting the Chilean military into an exclusive society, closed and apart. There is a descending scale of privileges, but even those at the bottom of the military ladder have their appetites for consumption and security satisfied. Not too many have access to the regime's big business deals, but even the lowliest member of the security forces is granted the means of improving his economic status.

He can permit prostitution, particularly by minors, in a sector of the city that he is assigned to patrol. He can authorize street vendors who trade in stolen or contraband goods. He can fine taxi drivers, or he can let them off. Everything has a price.

The Chilean economy is organized to benefit the generals and admirals and their protégés. Yet even the marginal areas of this country provide plenty of privileges for corporals and sergeants who already enjoy free housing, the education of their children, and stable employment.

They walk the cities of Chile in twos, or threes, or in two sets of pairs, at a slow pace. They are well dressed and well fed. Their uniforms are smart and comfortable. Their cheeks are well shaven, their black hair is cut short. They reply amiably to questions about the traffic, about places and distances; but their trained eyes focus on a face with precision. Small armored vehicles are stationed at strategic corners. Buses with reinforcements are parked nearby.

When everything is quiet—and it almost always is—Santiago resembles Paris during the early stages of the German occupation. You see the Paris of the newsreels of that time, the Paris of forever, with groups of two, three, or four German soldiers walking with a measured stride, confident about their future.

By November, spring is firmly established in Chile and by the twenty-fifth the evenings in Santiago are warm and the days hot. At 5 A.M. it is still dark, but this is the hour when Pinochet leaps out of bed to do his exercises. He tells the reporters who have called on him very early today that this awakening is an everyday occurrence and that three hours' sleep is all he needs. At seventy-one, with his gestures, his good humor, and his smiles, he is assuring the Chileans that they need have no fears about his energy and physical capabilities.

At 7:45 he begins to receive the greetings of all the authorities, functionaries, military chiefs, civilian dignitaries, delegations of corporals and sergeants, and low-level employees who are gathered in the Plaza de la Constitución in front of Government House to sing "Happy Birthday" to him. Pinochet comes out on the balcony to wave to them.

The Roman Catholic Church, most other Christian churches, and the rabbis do not take part in the celebrations. But a delegation of Mormon missionaries is present.

The military bands play serenades in the Plaza de la Constitución. The army band starts up, playing Pinochet's favorite tune, "Lili Marlene." In the Second World War it was the marching song of the army the General most admires. This admiration led the Pinochet government to censor the film *Cabaret* when it was released in Chile; scenes that showed the Nazis in an unfavorable light were cut.

This same day in Santiago Cathedral the cardinal is receiving a group of Catholic bishops from the United States. Seated in a semicircle around the cardinal's chair are all of Chile's religious leaders. The area in front of the cardinal is crowded with people of all kinds—from the poor who have come in from the outskirts of Santiago to a group of diplomats who have committed themselves to the defense of human rights.

They are celebrating a different anniversary. It is eight years since Pinochet's repression reached its peak in 1978, and the church leaders and the Grand Rabbi gave a solemn declaration. It was the Charter of Santiago and called upon the people to fight for human rights. The document was severely critical of the methods of the dictatorship.

From the pulpit a priest asks the representatives of the different groups to come forward and give two-minute answers to the same question: "What is your commitment to the defense of human rights, to the defense of life?" After each response there ring out the words "Glory, Glory Alleluia, in the Name of the Lord."

The lights are turned out, the huge wax candles are lit, as well as small candles in the hands of the congregants. Guitars play and the singing starts.

Once the diplomats, headed by the U.S. ambassador and the Swedish and Argentine chargés d'affaires, have departed to applause, the struggle begins between those who leave the cathedral shouting slogans against the repression and the carabineros, who lay about them with truncheons and water cannon.

Until nightfall the lawyers of the Vicariate of Solidarity, which was set up by the archbishopric, visit the hospitals and the police stations to identify the wounded and the detained, so that none of them "disappear."

2

Many Chileans kept themselves aloof. The vast majority went about their everyday business, tied to routine, like sleepwalkers. The Chileans call this form of evasion "submarining." They want to slip by, unnoticed, like submarines.

Submarining has taken the place of the spontaneity once so characteristic of Chileans.

The Chileans who remember the spontaneity explain that it was a product of the country's scenic beauty, the best poets in the Spanish-speaking world, splendid wines, and the most delicious seafood in the Pacific. A political club was called La Cuchara (The Spoon), because you had to eat well if you were going to talk politics. And because the world's best love poems were written by Pablo Neruda in the 1920s, all Chilean women are naturally beautiful and necessarily loved.

But submarining has gone on for many years, and much energy has been spent sniffing the air before accepting someone as a friend or even extending the limits of a conversation. You have to learn to "sniff" your neighbor, say Chileans. This means that when you meet people at a party, for example, you first have to determine whether the correct replies are given to a few questions, asked casually: what books have they read; where do they live (there are apartment buildings and neighborhoods exclusively for the military); what schools do their children attend (there are subsidized schools for the military and friends of the regime); what is their profession (there are professions, like psychology, that are barred from government positions); where do they shop (there are also subsidized supermarkets for the military).

The Chileans take pride in the fact that they have created an alternative life—a life despite the dictatorship, a life that is not without its moments of audacity. Of course, now and again, and in order not to become unbalanced, you need a touch of cynicism. That is what prompts Chileans to explain: "Chile is divided into two parts: the cowardly, who stayed, and the stupid, who left." If there were only the cowardly and the stupid, the alternative life would be a considerable achievement, a badge of merit, thanks to some hidden psychological mechanism. Life would go on. The human being would continue.

A country that has been isolated for so many years, while still eager to retain its identity and secure its survival, learns little from history, even from recent events. The Chileans know little about the Holocaust. They do not know how rich and full was the alternative life in the ghettos of Nazi-occupied Poland. During the Holocaust, the Jews managed to create a life with theaters, schools, choirs, lectures, chess tournaments, even beauty contests. Each time, after the Nazis had transported thousands to the gas chambers and the ovens of the crematoria, the alternative life continued—for those who remained.

Some Chilean psychologists who have dedicated themselves to looking after the victims of torture, the families of people who have disappeared, the exiles who have returned, and those who were uprooted from their homes believe that the alternative life is a creation of the regime—that the regime has had the intelligence to provide an escape valve for a system that, one way or another, has absorbed all levels of Chilean society.

People in the entertainment world in Santiago know that a study by experts advised the government that it would be wise to allow small theater groups to operate freely—tiny auditoriums, with 50 to 150 seats. The government experts, whom no one seems to know in person or even by name, are said to have calculated exactly how many people, and what type, attend these performances. They came to the conclusion that such audiences would not affect the government's stability, nor would they interfere with the norms of life imposed by the regime.

The experts are said to have gone even further in their calculations. They suggested that the participants in this alternative theater would fix their own limits for fear of going beyond the boundaries that they assumed had been set by the government. By making a mystery of these limits, the government has effectively forced the alternative theater, which is anxious to go on existing, to restrict itself. In this way, the government has succeeded in imposing a system of self-censorship designed to avert serious conflicts or controversies. The system has worked well for the regime.

A famous actor who is barred from appearing on television was allowed to make commercials promoting the very medium that had blacklisted him.

The alternative life was not only perfected by the regime itself, but the regime also found the means to force participants to render tribute to its demands, however irrational.

A group of writers and artists on the fringe of society, including some of the most sophisticated representatives of the alternative life, were loaned an old house, in terrible condition. They timidly began to organize a few cultural activities. They put on an exhibition by young unemployed artists. They sponsored poetry readings of unpublished works. There was a contest for short stories by political prisoners. The winning story was sent to Danielle Mitterrand, wife of the president of France. She responded with a moving letter which was posted on a wall of the building, and copies were distributed among the political prisoners.

It was then that toleration of the alternative life was briefly suspended. The door of the building opened violently and a bullet smashed into a stained-glass window above the stairway. The bullet hole is still there, a symbol of the limits of the alternative life. It is a scar, preserved with care by the artists, to show to visitors.

In 1985 three days were set aside for spontaneous and creative redecoration of the old building. Inside, two floors of the house were painted and decorated with murals and sculptures. There wasn't much furniture, but there were many sculptures. Performances of dance, music, and theater were organized to raise funds.

Authorization was sought from the mayor of Santiago to paint the outside of the building in lively colors and to incorporate some decorative designs. The mayor was reasonable: there must be no political figures, no political slogans, no historic figures who might be interpreted in a political sense. The artists understood perfectly. They could see that even the face of Jesus might be interpreted as support for the church in its struggle with the military regime. Depictions of Churchill or Eisenhower, who were victors over fascism, might be considered a call for the return of democracy in Chile. So they decided upon an abstract design.

They put up scaffolding, painted the outside walls, and then hit upon the idea of painting a long arrow which would begin on the roof, curl around the house, which is situated on a corner in front of a plaza, and finish on the ground. In its progress from the top of the house to the bottom, it would suggest the south. It would symbolize Chile, the country at the southernmost tip of the American continent.

The police arrested every one of the artists. The arrow, the regime had decided, had a hidden meaning—that of signifying the decline and fall of General Augusto Pinochet.

Between 1983 and 1986, when the economy had collapsed and the "economic miracle" had almost been forgotten, the misery of the people led to mass demonstrations in the streets. In the city of Santiago alone, the dictatorship sent 18,000 fully equipped troops into combat. Hitler's control of occupied France (with the help of the French police) needed no more. There were days when a hundred people died. There were days of fifty, ten, and three deaths. There were "disappearances." Bodies turned up with their throats cut.

Some demonstrators were burned to death, while some are still in jail or exile. The political leaders felt so strong that they called for the resignation of Pinochet, insisting on this as a precondition for their negotiating with the military. The leader of the Christian Democrats, the principal political party, proclaimed that 1986 was the decisive year for the removal of Pinochet. But they placed limits on the risks they were prepared to take and they were defeated. And so 1986 marked instead the consolidation of Pinochet. The appeal of the alternative life, which allowed opponents to go on living their evasive lives, was stronger than their convictions.

They returned to the alternative life. Not only did it offer a means of evasion, it also provided a source of income.

Prohibited from expressing themselves on television, artists began orchestrating an industry for the production of videocassettes. They brought together actors, dancers, directors, scene designers, musicians, composers. In tiny studios and theaters—sometimes in the street—they filmed documentaries, plays, experimental cinema, even theater in episodes. They were sold to those who owned video recorders—the major part of the middle class who had benefited from the "economic miracle"—and they were also sold in the democratic countries of the Spanish-speaking world. Television channels in Caracas, Buenos Aires, and Bogotá, as well as the Hispanic stations in the United States and in Madrid, were profitable markets for Chile's alternative TV.

The alternative life is full of creativity, because what is easy to do is prohibited. But it is a creativity that also generates the limitations that must be observed in order to survive. Few intellectuals and artists live fully the profundity of the crisis, with all its madness and its anxiety. They deal with essential themes with courage, but they do not break through them. It is notable that there is an absence of final consequences, which is precisely what defines a work of art. Perhaps artists will have to wait for their equivalent of the postwar years, as the Germans and the Italians did; or, like the Spanish, for the Chilean equivalent of the post-Franco period.

Nothing is easy because nothing is obvious. The government's actions cannot be predicted. It strikes swiftly and with impunity. It never gives explanations.

Perhaps what many people in Santiago believe is true: that the government has perfected the theory of the steam boiler. The alternative life is the steam the military allows to escape so that the boiler will not explode. Only Pinochet, however, knows when the valve should be opened and when it must be closed.

TESTIMONY

The whole time, approximately 16 days, they had me blindfolded. . . . Later they put electrodes on my toes, knees, the tip of my penis and on my testicles. . . . Every night, except for the last two, they made me sleep standing up. Every other day they would hang me and beat me. They had a barometer: it was that blood would burst from my nose and ears. I saw that when I felt something hot drip from my nose and ears, they would calm down and lower me.

Around the fourth day they showed me a rat and it seems I showed an adverse reaction, because they then forced a rat into my mouth, into my shorts, closing all the exits, and into my pants, with the ends sealed by my socks. . . . We went directly from the Central Nacional de Informaciones location to the Military Prosecutor, just moments after being tortured. For the first time, in the doorway of the Prosecutor's office, I had my blindfold removed.

(Testimony of the actor Sergio Buschmann, presented by Americas Watch Committee, New York)

3

The barrio of Bellavista appears to have ended its exile. Memories of the long night, of deep and murderous darkness, are gradually fading away. In September 1973, the military found in the student hostels of Bellavista, in the studios of artists and writers, in the art galleries, in the little theaters, hundreds of tempting victims.

In Bellavista, on a hill separated from the center of the city by the Mapocho River, stood the house of Pablo Neruda. The military took it by assault—it was empty at the time—and they destroyed furniture and collections of miniatures brought back by the poet from his journeys in Thailand, China, Peru, Romania. They stole gifts presented to him by Pablo Picasso. They thrust their bayonets into almost all the paintings and left behind only objects whose value they could not appreciate. A painting by Fernand Léger was saved, as was a work by Diego Rivera. A collection of small statues of ancient Chinese warriors, made of painted terra-cotta, disappeared. The peasant ceramics he had brought from Poland were destroyed. So were the black ceramics that Neruda had found in the south of Chile, in Quinchamallí. All the primitive paintings collected patiently in journeys through Chile, Colombia, and Mexico, to Samarkand and Bokhara, vanished. His collection of tiny antique clocks was also stolen. The huge clock above the fireplace was smashed and left in pieces. Something about the nose of the subject in a portrait by a pupil of Caravaggio aroused the curiosity of the military, because they pierced it with a bayonet. They set a fire in part of the house and blocked a canal that flowed down the hill. That flooded the rest of Neruda's home.

When Neruda returned from his long journeys or exile to Isla Negra on the Pacific Coast, to La Sebastiana in the port of Valparaíso, or to La Chascona in Bellavista, he used to say: "I have returned from my voyages. I navigated constructing happiness." A few days after the military coup, in September 1973, following the burning of his house in Bellavista, Pablo Neruda was mourned there—his corpse lay between the ruins and the flood.

In 1986, in the thirteenth year of the Pinochet era, Bellavista took advantage of the options that the regime allows. They are small options, but in the soft temperate spring nights, with all the windows open, the tree-lined streets were filled with songs, young voices reading poetry, the murmur of discussions and infinite conversations in cafés and restaurants.

Those who returned from exile have much to ask. Those who stayed have much to tell. They are tender encounters, but hardly happy ones.

She says, without special emphasis, that she knew repression existed in the same way that one is aware of death. But she says that no one ever thinks that the time to die has arrived. That is how she lived in Chile under the military.

Yet it was necessary to create support systems in order not to despair. For example, there is this exorcism: "I am not like those they killed; I am not like those who are imprisoned." You can also weigh your activities to convince yourself that the things that you do cannot seriously affect the regime. To believe yourself innocent is also a form of exorcism.

Nevertheless, there are moments of panic when exorcism does not work. Then it is a sound idea to take a walk, or lose yourself among the trees in a park, or go to the cinema. Relax.

She is a Chilean aristocrat. She knows how to converse in the appropriate way, with allusions in English and French. In this small seafood restaurant in Bellavista, she knows how to order the same wine and food she had in the stately mansion of her adolescence. The only thing she has forgotten is that a lady must always—almost always—smile to cover up any tension and avoid a hard facial expression. She is not tense, but quiet and calm. She has huge almond-shaped eyes and an elongated face, like almost everyone in her family. But she does not smile.

As well as exorcism, there is fantasy. You can earn a green belt at karate and, perhaps, avert being kidnapped in the street. You feel that in some circumstances you might be able to defend yourself. But she did not take the course in karate. There are those who force themselves to attend the weekly lessons. She does not.

You can put an alarm system in your house to avoid any unexpected entrance. But the men who install it might inform the police. There would be questions. In any case, why do so? She has not been very active during these past thirteen years of fear. Personal and collective fear. Individual fear. Fear for your children. Fear for your friends. She did sign some declarations about human rights, sponsored by the Catholic Church. She wrote some short stories, but there was no hate, no denunciation in them. She divorced a man of her class to marry a man who had returned from exile, a return authorized by the government. This cannot signify guilt. Fully a million of Chile's 11 million population went into exile, and a great many of them have returned.

When they knocked at her door, all the exorcism and fantasy failed. She opened the door and right there, in the street, they beat her savagely.

It was nothing more than that. They hit her and hit her. There were no accusations or warnings. Just punches and kicks. Blows.

The lack of significance was more painful than the blows because it left so many questions open. The exorcism and the fantasy were no use. All that was left was fear and the discovery that it could happen to anyone at any moment.

She took her children to the house of her ex-husband. They had maintained a good relationship, and met and talked frequently. They went on seeing their children and sharing in their education. That was all. She found some consolation, like so many Chileans do when everything collapses under the repression. She knew that her husband had merely to appear before a judge—one of Pinochet's judges—and he would be given custody of the children. Throughout the first thirteen years of the dictatorship this happened in case after case affecting divorced couples of her class. Many obtained divorces with political denunciations—some true, some false. They also acquired property rights and custody of the children. Her husband did not do this. It is a consolation.

The apparent irrationality in the repression carried out by the Chilean military conforms in reality to a scheme worked out by experts and analyzed by Bruno M. Bettelheim:

> . . . the terror the concentration camps created was made even more effective by the utterly arbitrary manner in which the Gestapo imprisoned some and set others free. There was no way to guess why one prisoner was let go after a few months, when another just like him was released only after several years, and yet another was doomed to remain forever in the camps.

The fact that Pinochet is considered to be part of the Western world, the good ally of the United States, whose rise to power was achieved through the good offices of Richard Nixon and Henry Kissinger, does not mean that the regime will discard Nazi methods of repression.

Not everyone has learned to live in Pinochet's Chile. In 1985, during the celebration of Passover, the holy days when the Jews remember their escape from slavery in Egypt, the Grand Rabbi of Chile described Pinochet as the new Pharaoh. Subsequently, a bomb attack was directed against a leader of the synagogue. The Rabbi was not expelled from the country, because he had become a Chilean citizen after the leader of a Protestant church, a European who had retained his citizenship, was taken to the airport and deported. The Grand Rabbi thereby not only evaded expulsion but also neutralized criticism from the traditional leaders of the Jewish community, who had denounced him as a foreigner—he is Argentine—and accused him of interfering in the internal affairs of Chile. The Grand Rabbi today works with human rights organizations, calls for the freeing of political prisoners, protests torture. The leaders of the temple forced him to resign, but he organized another synagogue.

Those who tried to establish a sophisticated dialogue with the military at the highest levels ran into difficulties—but that is all. An ordinary Chilean who approached two carabineros on street patrol and presented them with a bunch of flowers to open a conversation was arrested. For the judge who convicted him there was no room for doubt: he was guilty of attempting to bribe them and of offending the dignity of the carabinero corps.

Someone enters a public lavatory. He reads, in a loud voice, an anti-Pinochet inscription on the wall. The judge condemns him to five years internal exile in a desolate spot.

Others learn. A lawyer of the Catholic Church's Vicariate of Solidarity called on all his neighbors and explained what they should do and what he and his family would do if there was an attempt to kidnap him.

The cars arrived during the night at the lawyer's old house, which had been built almost like a fortress by a German immigrant at the beginning of the century. They came through the garden, but the two sturdy doors, one at the front of the house and one leading into the kitchen, were both reinforced with steel bars. The doors stood up to the first assault. Then, when the attackers tried to get through the windows, which had iron bars, the lawyer and his family turned on all the lights in the house, blew whistles, and clanged cooking pots.

The attackers tried to force the iron bars on the windows, but the lights in the other houses in the neighborhood were now turned on and the neighbors were banging cooking pots and blowing whistles. Five minutes later the hooded attackers left in their dark cars. The operators at the local telephone exchange reported that emergency calls to the archbishopric, foreign correspondents, and the embassies of the United States, Argentina and Sweden, reporting what was going on, had been intercepted.

There have been others who have learned to live in Chile, although it has taken them a long time to perfect their methods. In September 1983, after a decade of military repression, thousands killed and imprisoned, and seven hundred documented "disappeared," some seventy-five people gathered in front of a police investigations center that was supposed to be secret. They unfurled a banner: "Here they are torturing a man." In silence, each person pointed an index finger at the building. They were beaten and they were dispersed, but a new movement had adopted the slogan of an Argentine who himself had been tortured in Buenos Aires, the Nobel Peace Prize laureate Adolfo Pérez Esquivel. His slogan is: "Nonviolence is also a rebellion against oppression." With time, they learned much more. They now number three hundred and they have adopted the name of Sebastián Acevedo, a citizen who committed suicide in front of the cathedral in the city of Concepción. He set fire to himself. He was asking that his two children, who had been kidnapped by the military forty-eight hours earlier, appear alive.

The Sebastián Acevedo Movement accepts as members only those who believe in nonviolence as a doctrine and do not look upon it merely as a tactic. To avoid infiltration, only those who are recommended by a member of the movement are considered for membership.

Members believe that the military's use of torture is the Achilles' heel of the dictatorship and that by denouncing it they will eventually not only overthrow the military but also bring them to trial and ultimately found a new moral order in Chile.

They accept relatives of torture victims as well as family

members of political prisoners. They also encourage relatives of disappeared people to join. But they will not admit anyone who has suffered torture. The reason is that a torture victim might break down under the tension that builds up during street demonstrations.

A detailed study is made beforehand of each place they plan to expose. They find out at what time of day it is most crowded so that their demonstration will have maximum impact. They calculate the number of policemen who patrol the area and work out how long it will take for the troop carriers and trucks with water cannon to reach the spot from the nearest military garrison. They also try to stage their protests at an hour of the day when heavy traffic is likely to delay the antiriot squads en route.

On the night prior to each demonstration, members of the movement meet in small groups for reflection and prayer. The road of nonviolence is not an easy one to travel; those who take it know that they themselves will be the target of violence. They see themselves as tiny drops of water splashing on the stone of the dictatorship, but the stone, even if it is wearing away, strikes back brutally.

They take chains and padlocks and shackle themselves to the iron railings of a public building. They do not shout or sing. Then they unroll their sign denouncing torture, and while the police hit them and douse them with water they pray in silence. They know that passersby who see them will be afraid to become involved, but that they will report what they have observed and that their information—although censored by the mass media—will travel by word of mouth to every corner of Chile.

One hundred of them arrive, one by one, for a demonstration outside the offices of the Chilean Medical Association in Santiago. Their sign calls upon the Association to expel those physicians who cooperate with police torturers.

Outside *El Mercurio,* Chile's leading newspaper, they lie down in the street so that it will take the police longer to disperse them. Their sign reads: "In Chile they torture, but *El Mercurio* says nothing."

They gather outside the Palacio de la Moneda (Government

House) in the Plaza de la Constitución. There are only twenty of them, and they have already calculated that it will take seven minutes for the guards to reach them. They set up a sign that reads "Yes to life; no to torture" and disperse quickly.

On the day set aside to honor the carabineros, different groups call at police stations to deliver letters expressing regret that the once respected national police is "not the institution it was because we know that it is now guilty of torture." Many of the demonstrators are beaten, but members of the movement believe that there must be a decent man inside each uniform and that one day they will be able to communicate with him. So far, however, they have achieved very little. In a few isolated instances policemen, when they think they are not being watched by their officers, will not mistreat the Acevedo members. There are also occasional cases in which women are told to scream as if they were being raped but, in the darkness of their cells, are not harmed. These too few cases keep the hopes of the movement alive, but the members do not have many illusions: in Chile there is torture every day and at every hour of the day.

At Christmas, movement members went from church to church passing out handwritten cards with this greeting: "For a Christmas without Herods and a New Year without torturers." When one was arrested, the entire group insisted on being detained as well.

A Catholic priest is their spiritual adviser. It is he who, on the night prior to each demonstration, finds the words that will calm them a little and allow them to snatch a few hours of sleep. It is the priest who points out to them that the idea sustaining the Sebastián Acevedo Movement is in the teachings of St. Thomas Aquinas, Gandhi, and Pope John XXIII: that nonviolence is active rebellion.

TESTIMONY

I am 18 years old. I was arrested on September 4 at about midday. At the time I was traveling in a taxi with my boyfriend to a friend's house. Suddenly we were intercepted by a truck full of soldiers who surrounded us, violently pulled us out of the taxi and made us stand against a wall. There they fondled me in an obscene manner while the officer in charge shouted insults at me. A large group of civilians arrived and started beating me. Then they put me into a car, blindfolded me and applied electric shocks to my back. The vehicle set off and I was taken to a house where they beat my parents and my 15-year-old brother. They got me out of the car and beat me with the butts of their weapons, put me back in the car and then drove me to a place I could not identify because of the blindfold. There they made me take a pill and began to interrogate me, insulting me and shouting at me. At the same time they applied electric shocks to my breasts. They asked me for names and addresses. Then they took me to a room where they stripped me and tied me to a bed. One of them raped me and then made me get dressed. Afterwards I was again made to get into a car and taken to a place that, from its appearance, seemed to be the Central Nacional de Informaciones detention center in Borgoño Street. My clothes were exchanged for overalls of lightweight cloth and shoes made of the same material. They took me to a room where they made me lie down on a bedframe. I was examined by a man they called a doctor. There were also two women and underneath my blindfold I could see they were dressed in white. The doctor listened to my heart and measured my blood pressure and pulse. . . .

Each day I was there, except the last two, I was interrogated using the same methods, and each day I was examined by a doctor and made to take pills several times. They made me sign about fourteen sheets of paper, putting my fingerprints on each one. I was not allowed to read the contents, so I don't know what was written on them.

(Testimony of student Patricia Peña Diaz, presented by Amnesty International, London. She discovered she was pregnant as a result of the rape. She lost the baby after two months.)

4

Near Calama, some thousand miles from Santiago, there are a number of small, indigenous settlements. The men are miners. The women work the inhospitable, dry, windswept desert land.

Men were taken from their homes in October 1973 and were shot by order of a general who arrived by helicopter. In the helicopter was a young officer, Armando Fernandez Larios, who, years later, was involved in the automobile bombing in Washington, D.C., that killed Orlando Letelier, who had been Salvador Allende's foreign minister.

The military returned to the houses of the men they had shot, and threatened the women. They were told that they must never speak about what had happened—if they did, their children would be killed.

The Women of Calama, as they are called today, organized their lives around silence. Some, the most daring among them, placed photographs of their husbands on abandoned graves in small dusty cemeteries. Once a year, and always in silence, they would take their children to the purported graves to keep their memories alive. But they never knew and never inquired what had really happened to their men-folk.

Other mothers simply told their children to be patient, because their fathers had left in search of work.

Every so often a military officer would return to check the area; but the Women of Calama never broke their silence. They lived precariously off the land, like their forebears through the centuries; they had always suffered in silence. These women had now been commanded to subsist and keep silent; but their lives had always been ones of bare subsistence and of silence.

It appeared that what had happened to the Women of Calama was a perfect example of the dictatorship achieving its objective: the total silence of its victims. But silence is not always complicity.

There was much misery in the early years of the Pinochet regime. Later, however, there was a bigger market for fruit and vegetables, some cheeses, and even for the textiles that were woven in the traditional Indian manner. The Women of Calama knew next to nothing about the so-called economic boom that Chile was enjoying. They knew even less about the accumulating foreign debt. Neither had they any idea of the availability of color television sets and imported automobiles with which the regime sought, and achieved, the corruption of the middle class. But more food, more clothes, and even some new furniture reached Calama.

The helicopter that brought the general and his men to the area landed first at La Serena on October 16, 1973—some five weeks after the military coup—and on this same day, at four o'clock in the afternoon, fifteen people were executed. On October 17 they moved on to Copiapó and another thirteen people were shot. The military reached Antofagasta on the eighteenth, and on the morning of the nineteenth they killed eighteen political prisoners. They flew on to Calama, where, at five o'clock in the afternoon, twenty-six political prisoners were taken from their cells and shot.

Among the twenty-six were journalists, lawyers, engineers, and mine officials. Their widows and children denounced the executions and protested from that day onward. But the peasants weren't aware of the story of the helicopter. They had never heard of human rights organizations and didn't know how to make denunciations or how to protest. They went to church to pray, but they never confided their secret to the priest. They knew that thanks to their silence their children were still alive. People exchanged few words even in normal times, so no questions were asked, no explanations expected.

The first person in the outside world to hear what had happened at Calama was a psychologist who attended one of the women at a social service clinic. The woman needed treatment for a nervous disorder. The psychologist was in touch with a group of psychoanalysts in Santiago who were working in the offices of the United Nations High Commissioner for Refugees under the sponsorship of the Christian Churches' Social Aid Foundation.

In the therapy they have developed for individual victims of repression, the psychoanalysts have confirmed what Bruno Bettelheim had established in his studies of the Nazi concentration camps: survival was intimately linked to the ability of the individual to find some significance in his situation based on his knowledge, his ideology, or his political or religious beliefs. This certainly did not apply to the primitive, long-suffering women of Calama.

The psychoanalysts also discovered something new: the repression in Chile is designed to cause psychological damage to vast sectors of the population. This means that there should be some form of collective treatment for all Chileans. It can be done by providing information about what has happened, by explaining it and, in this way, alleviating the entire population from the damaging consequences of a mass trauma. The trauma is characterized by two psychic disorders. First is the total negation of actual experience, which leads to difficulty in evaluating everyday events because of a "black hole" in the memory. Then there is the sense of guilt felt by those who have survived.

The political conditions for collective therapy for a public psychosis obviously do not exist in Chile today. In dealing with individual cases, the psychiatrists have established the various states that are repeated most frequently in the thousands of patients who can attend therapy sessions. They are depression, anxiety, insomnia, nightmares, diminution of intellectual powers, difficulties in sexual functioning, changes in family and emotional relationships, apathy, loss of memory, frigidity, lack of interest. In the case of the Women of Calama, the psychiatrists discovered something else: an unresolved state of mourning and the fear of more horror in the future. Similar situations had been detected in relatives of disappeared people, who felt a sense of guilt about going on living because of an inability to mourn the missing person. The fear of more horror affects an enormous spectrum of people, ranging from those who have been tortured and threatened with more torture if they divulge what they have seen in prison, to those whose fears stem simply from having seen someone arrested.

The psychiatrists also discovered a tactical decision made by the military: that all women arrested for political reasons should be raped. In those days the rapes were mostly carried out by the military themselves, but specially trained dogs were also often used to violate women prisoners. The analysts point out that a rapist is an abnormal person, but the individual who worked out this particular tactic was an intelligent and cultivated man who knew that a woman who has been raped faces great difficulties in rebuilding her emotional life afterwards. He realized, too, that for wives and mothers a sense of humiliation would permeate family life, causing permanent emotional instability. Additionally, the use of rape as simply another police method—a routine part of the system—was a way of overcoming any resistance by the police themselves. A student of biochemistry testified that the man ordered to rape her objected, but was forced to do so by the other carabineros, who then proceeded to gang-rape her. The wife of a judicial official heard of a policeman who refused to slash a cross on the breast of a woman because she reminded him of his own mother, but he was forced to do so.

In the years of military dictatorship not a single rapist has been brought to trial or even reprimanded. Not one military man has apparently felt that his code of honor or his conviction that an officer is always a gentleman has been affected by the routine rape of women prisoners. Neither has the Christian faith of any officer been in conflict, it seems, with the fact that every pregnant woman who is arrested is beaten and tortured until she loses her baby.

The case of the Women of Calama was not unique. Their passivity, their fears that the killers might return, the creation of the illusory graves to which they could take flowers and the long years that passed in silence have been repeated elsewhere.

It was the identification of the victims of the firing squad in Calama that began the unraveling of the women's secret. Of the twenty-six men shot in Calama, there were some who had never been involved in political or social activities. The reasons for their arrest and execution, if there were any, remained a complete mystery. Nobody asked about them. There were no protests from any political party, labor union, or even any family member. They were just men.

The psychologists investigating the executions went in search of the widows. A slow, difficult process of collective and individual therapy began. Distrust had to be overcome, safety guaranteed. The truth had to be shared with the children. The rite of mourning—beginning with the acceptance of death and the manner in which death had occurred, and with all the pain of remembering—had to be observed. The family unit, in which identities had been mutilated and the natural role of each member had been altered, had to be reconstructed. It was also necessary to establish a clear idea of a possible future and, above all, to eliminate fear.

Avoiding the creation of resentment within the family unit because of what happened on that night in 1973 was also important. The mothers might feel resentment toward their children because they had maintained silence to protect the children's lives, and then internalize this resentment as a betrayal of their husbands. The children, on the other hand, might feel resentment for having been lied to about the fate of their fathers. For many years the children had been forbidden to cry. It was not easy to find out how they had kept their feelings about the disappearance or death of their fathers private and how they had assimilated the terror they had sensed in their mothers.

Eradicating fear and ending anxiety about more horror in

the future was, perhaps, the most difficult stage in the therapy. The problem gave rise to a conference of psychologists in Buenos Aires on "The Culture of Fear in Totalitarian Regimes."

The psychologists established the following general characteristics of a state of constant fear:

Sensation of vulnerability: In the face of life-threatening situations there is a sense of personal weakness. The individual feels "identified" and "persecuted" and loses all possibility of privacy and intimacy in his personal life. He becomes susceptible to arbitrary behavior beyond his control.

State of alert: The senses are exacerbated and the individual cannot rest in the face of imminent danger and the life-threatening situation this poses. This can be expressed in various symptomatic ways.

Individual impotence: The individual recognizes that his own resources and strength are inadequate to deal with adversity. The individual in this situation feels he has no control over his own life and that decisions about his future are not in his hands. This impotence, and the allied feelings of vulnerability and helplessness, give rise to a sense of abandonment in the face of violence.

Alteration of the sense of reality: As one of the objectives of inducing fear is to deprive an individual of his ability to act, the ordinary sense of reality is deliberately disrupted and rendered useless. It comes to seem practically impossible to verify what is objective fact as against subjective experience, and the boundary between what is real and possible on the one hand and what is fantasy and imagination on the other tends to dissolve. Reality becomes confusing and threatening, with no clear borders, and so loses its guiding role in subjective processes.

New fears emerged. Each member of each family had developed mechanisms to adapt to the situation and each was afraid he might not find suitable substitutes.

The psychologists decided that the conclusion of this first stage of the treatment of the Calama families should take the form of a celebration in which the most painful aspects of their experience were to be alleviated. The families had to be reconciled with the murder of their menfolk and reconciled with fear. The ceremony would be outspoken and undisguised. Afterwards individual therapy could continue.

The celebration was in the cemetery with all the women, their children, friends, neighbors, and psychologists, and the photographs of the murdered men who were to receive symbolic burial. They told stories to each other, they all shared food prepared by the women themselves, and there were musicians to accompany the singing.

They spent the day talking, remembering the past and revealing themselves, trying to come to terms with reality and with each other. Singing songs with familiar words was also good therapy.

Bruno Bettelheim has entitled one of his essays "The Ultimate Limit," a title that comes from a verse by Horace: *Mors ultima linea rerum est* ("Death is the ultimate limit of things").

In Calama, at the celebration of Calama, death ceased to be an ending and became a beginning.

More than Horace, the dead of Calama recall the verses of Francisco de Quevedo, the Spanish poet of the seventeenth century:

> *They will be ashes, but with meaning;*
> *Dust they'll be, but dust in love.*

TESTIMONY

I shouted and screamed like an animal from the intensity of the pain, and the method they used; it was like tweezers were being applied to my testicles. Crusts and scabs formed on my mouth and I couldn't speak. I had to tear them off with my hands. . . . I noticed that my testicles were bleeding. My penis, testicles, and part of the gland were torn open and all bloody. . . . Then they took me to a cell where my son was detained and they beat him in front of me. . . . Later they said they had knocked down my other son who is six and that he was dead. . . . After that they told me that they were going to torture my daughter, that they would open her up and leave her menstruating for the rest of her life. . . .

(Testimony of José Abelardo Moya, presented by Americas Watch Committee, New York)

5

There is a simple question that is being asked in Chile today: How can we bring Pinochet's dictatorship to an end? Answers range from the frank ingenuousness of José Donoso, Chile's greatest contemporary writer, who, speaking of the United States, said: "They put him in, so they should take him out," to the assassination attempt organized by the Communist Party. It would be impossible to list all the solutions Chileans have imagined that fall between these two extremes or capture the nuances of the various proposals.

Lyndon Johnson and Richard Nixon were the two U.S. presidents in office when Chile made its only serious attempts, within a legal, constitutional framework, to modify an economic and social structure that condemned the country to backwardness and underdevelopment. Johnson did not understand the "revolution in liberty" that President Eduardo Frei, the Christian Democrat, was trying to achieve. President Nixon would not accept Salvador Allende's "peaceful road to socialism," even though it had been accepted by Chileans and their leaders in free elections.

There is little that Chileans do not know about the continuous intervention of the United States to obstruct both Frei's and Allende's reforms. If they need to understand any more about the political mechanisms employed by Washington or about the influence over the White House of the U.S. companies that exploited Chile's copper, they will find it in the 25,000 words that Seymour M. Hersh devotes to Chile in his book *The Price of Power: Kissinger in the Nixon White House.*

From this perspective, it is easy to understand Donoso's ingenuous remark. Yet in its policy toward Chile, the United States has run into a snag it has encountered many times before. The U.S. does not always know how to remove those it has placed in power, or whether it should do so.

It is true that political assassination in Latin America is not excluded from consideration by the White House. On more than one occasion the idea of killing Salvador Allende—either before he took office or while he was president—passed through the fevered brains of Washington's operators. But Pinochet is now too well guarded for that.

There is certainly nothing repugnant to Washington in the idea of eliminating a right-wing dictator who has enjoyed its backing and flattery—take, for example, the demise of General Rafael Leónidas Trujillo in the Dominican Republic in 1961. The physical elimination of the dictator was planned to provide support for Romulo Betancourt, the president of Venezuela (whom Trujillo had been harassing), in a confrontation with Fidel Castro.

Among the many Chileans who believe that it is vitally necessary to eliminate Pinochet, the majority would prefer to see the United States accomplish this, rather than the Communists. As they see it, the Chilean armed forces would accept the deed if it were carried out by Washington, whereas terrible, indiscriminate repression would be unleashed if the Communists were to assassinate Pinochet, and this would serve to consolidate the military regime.

However, the United States seems to have other plans for Chile. This time they are not violent, as they were with Nixon and Kissinger. Washington's ideas are also far removed from the magic world that Chilean politicians dream about—an "Operation Chile" to remove Pinochet that would be over in twenty-four hours. The preferred U.S. scenario is that the Chilean armed forces themselves bring the Pinochet dictatorship to a close—peacefully and, if possible, within the legal framework of the regime. Pinochet would be allowed to spend the rest of his days in a country of his choice and the political parties would be expected to permit the military to return to their barracks in peace and the Chilean Communist Party would be isolated.

Although the proposal is simple, carrying it out would not be. Pinochet is maneuvering all the time, he is extremely good at political maneuvering, and he has his own friends in Washington, notably Senator Jesse Helms and the former ambassador to the United Nations, Jeanne Kirkpatrick. For their part, the political parties still have no common objective, even after a decade and a half of dictatorship. It is surprising that they have managed to unite in alliances, in research institutes, in coalitions, in street demonstrations, and in deciding strategies; they have been together in jails, in exile, in the underground resistance; yet they have never learned that they must sacrifice what may seem to be a benefit for their party in pursuit of a common objective.

What Washington has achieved in a short time, merely by changing its attitude and changing to an ambassador who is not afraid to be critical of the regime, is that for the first time in Latin America the intervention of the United States is accepted—with enthusiasm or with resignation. Pinochet's authoritarian personality and the savagery of the military repression in Chile have contributed enormously to the sanction of U.S. intervention.

There can surely be no precedent in Latin America for a conference of political leaders on relations with the United States that has not been converted into a platform for denouncing U.S. imperialism. Yet, toward the end of 1986, in the headquarters of the professional association of journalists (Colegio de Periodistas) in Santiago, a panel of political leaders from the right, left, and center discussed, seriously, rationally, and with equanimity, the possible participation of Washington in the overthrow of Pinochet and the U.S. role in a period of transition to democracy. The topic was "Prospects for American Policy towards Chile" and, naturally, the major complaints came from the left, but they were not the traditional, virulent global attacks on imperialist policies. Instead, viewing the situation almost with sadness, the left lamented that the United States intervenes only in cases of crisis and that, unfortunately, it does not perceive a crisis in Chile so far.

Washington achieved this consensus over a period of two years by its almost constant criticism of human rights violations in Chile and by calling for the lifting of restrictions on press freedom.

Of course, there are other explanations for U.S. policy toward Chile that Chileans put forward during their incessant debates. Some of these explanations give rise to ambivalent, guilty feelings. For example, there exists a suspicion that the strategy of the United States toward Chile is linked to its policy toward Nicaragua. This theory holds that the overthrow of Pinochet would clear the way for the marines to invade Nicaragua and to bomb Managua, all the while arguing that the struggle against dictatorship in Latin America must be against left- as well as right-wing regimes. The Chileans do not reject the theory but, because they are desperate about their own situation, they try to bury it in the depths of their subconscious.

The explanation advanced by Chile's innumerable political scientists—the largest number per capita in Latin America—mixes confidential information with a great deal of speculation. They claim that the presidents of two leading democracies, Jaime Lusinchi of Venezuela and Raúl Alfonsín of Argentina, contrived to convince Ronald Reagan that Pinochet's continuance in power would increase Cuban and Soviet involvement in Chile. They also cite a so-called Ponomarev report, said to have originated in the Kremlin, which contains three main points:

1. The Communist Party opposed Fidel Castro in the 1950s when he called for an armed struggle in Cuba against Fulgencio Batista. The party called him a bourgeois adventurer. The Communists managed to gain power and maintain their influence because, in his first year, Castro refused to give in to the demands of the Eisenhower administration. The Kremlin acted swiftly to fill the vacuum.

2. In Nicaragua the Communist Party accused the Sandinistas of being adventurers and opposed their guerrilla tactics. The Nicaraguan Communists did not participate in the overthrow of Anastasio Somoza and are still out of power, despite the fact that the country is surviving on Soviet and Cuban aid.

3. In Chile, according to the report, neither of these two situations must be repeated. The Communist Party must try, with the help of the Soviet Union and Cuba, to be the principal factor, if not the only one, in the overthrow of Pinochet by insurrection.

Presidents Lusinchi and Alfonsín are said to have insisted in separate conversations with Reagan that a civil war in Chile would lead to the participation of contingents from all the countries of Latin America and the almost inevitable military intervention of the United States. The entire continent would be affected and the stability of the democracies in Latin America would be seriously threatened. For Argentina, where democracy has been so recently restored, the civil war would mean a 5,000-kilometer frontier of mountains and forests across which the flow of arms and men could not be prevented. It could also mean the almost certain intervention of the Argentine armed forces in defiance of the civilian government, which obviously would declare Argentina's neutrality.

The Chileans soon saw corroboration of this explanation of the situation in two events. One was the clandestine arrival of a huge amount of Soviet weapons, dropped off by ship on the northern Pacific coast, and the other was the assassination attempt on Pinochet by Chilean Communists who had been trained abroad.

The failure of the two operations—the most serious interventions ever carried out by Cuba and the Soviet Union in any country in the "southern cone" of Latin America—accelerated a crisis that had been brewing in the heart of the Communist Party and in its relations with the democratic parties in opposition to Pinochet. Finally, in December 1986, the Chilean Communists renounced the insurrectionary, terrorist policy line in an official document that was also signed by a socialist group and an extreme left-wing Christian movement. Of course, this renunciation does not rule out the possibility of other terrorist acts by splinter groups of militants, or of the Communists abrogating the new policy and resuming such activity.

The Castro and Sandinista models for overthrowing the regime are rejected by the vast majority of Chileans. Other options for removing military governments that have been tried in other parts of Latin America in recent years seem only distant possibilities, if not impossibilities, to the Chileans.

In Argentina, a war with Britain which was started by the military ended in ignominious defeat and brought down the dictatorship after almost eight years in power. It was not battlefield defeat as such that finally crushed and discredited the armed forces. The Argentine people had welcomed the invasion of the Islas Malvinas (as the Argentines call the Falkland Islands) in April 1982 because this tiny archipelago is deeply embedded in the national consciousness. They would have accepted an honorable defeat. But the dictatorship claimed that it had beaten the English and was only awaiting their surrender. The military leaders publicized this imaginary victory for weeks on end. The defeat was revealed only after the Argentine troops on the islands had themselves surrendered. This anticlimax aroused more indignation than the armed forces could bear. The military leaders sought any means available to escape from this situation and realized that the one way they could ease the public pressure was to call for elections. In their panic they failed to negotiate their own future. The public's discovery of the incapacity, corruption, and ineptitude that characterized the invasion of the Falkland Islands thwarted the military from imposing the amnesty they had decreed to protect themselves from being brought to justice under a civilian administration. The military leaders were divided, ashamed, confused, frightened, and humiliated.

It is impossible for Pinochet to fall into the same error, particularly after the Argentine debacle. Chile has no territorial claims. On the contrary, in wars during the past century Chile acquired both Peruvian and Bolivian territory. Any possibility of achieving democracy by the military's being defeated in a war with another country is quite out of the question.

In Brazil, Peru, and Uruguay, the military leaders ran out of objectives and, in each case, the dictatorship negotiated a return to democracy. The military regime lasted twenty years in Brazil and almost fifteen years in Peru and Uruguay. In Chile, the dictatorship has not run out of objectives. In fact, the regime has a plan to perpetuate itself which, because it can be imposed by force, could be successful.

Under the constitution approved by plebiscite in 1980, General Pinochet will continue as head of state until March 1989, after elections are held for a new president. The plebiscite bore scant resemblance to a democratic vote, but the armed forces will not allow even a shadow of doubt to fall on its legitimacy. The constitution establishes that the elections will take the form of a plebiscite with only one candidate and only one option: "yes" or "no." The sole candidate will be selected by the armed forces themselves before December 1988. If a majority votes "no" in the plebiscite, then there will be a "free" election a year later—but without the participation of Marxist parties. As the military's definition of "Marxist" is not easy to interpret, there is no knowing how free the elections will be.

From the moment the 1980 constitution was sanctioned, political life in Chile has been a sad comedy of tangled relations and tragic ambiguity. The political leadership has not come up with a strategy despite the many highly sophisticated projects that have been worked out. As a result, the Chilean people have had to pay, and to go on paying, a very high price.

The most important collective actions jointly decided by the political leaders have been the mass demonstrations that have taken place since 1983. The political leaders convinced themselves that they could make Chile appear ungovernable and so persuade the armed forces to replace Pinochet and negotiate a transition to democracy with them.

The leaders also managed to convince the Chilean people that such a strategy was possible. Throughout the country, people took to the streets or barricaded themselves in their neighborhoods. They accepted hundreds of deaths and thousands of prisoners and torture victims in the belief that 1986 would be the decisive year in the struggle to overthrow Pinochet. The battles and sacrifices lasted three years and, as time passed, they became a source of frustration and disillusionment. Chileans proved what had already been demonstrated in Argentina, Brazil, and Uruguay—that in any major Latin American nation, only the armed forces themselves can bring down a military government. Pinochet's strength with the military reached a peak after the discovery of the Cuban and Soviet arsenals and in the wake of the attempt on his life. Yet some sectors of public opinion, including groups on the right and even military commanders, began to question his psychological stability when the police kidnapped and murdered four people, failing in their attempt to abduct a fifth, as vengeance for the five bodyguards killed in the assassination attempt. It was an unrestrained act of revenge.

During the mass demonstrations Pinochet showed the armed forces that the country was not ungovernable; but after the response to the attempt on his life, some military leaders realized that the old general was unpredictable.

You sense in the Chileans the anguish they feel over the infinite number of answers the politicians give to the same question: What is the way out?

The answer is not to be found in Chile's twenty-three universities. The military regime has disrupted the universities and lowered their academic standards. It was particularly merciless with professors and students in the fields of political science and social studies.

The alternative life—the contradictory search for creative space within a dictatorship—gave birth to about fifty high-level research institutes and private study centers and to several dozen organizations at a somewhat lower level. There isn't a political tendency or ideological outlook, or a religious or philosophic discipline, that is not represented in one of these think tanks. And there is not a single aspect of Chilean reality that is overlooked in all this research activity.

Working in the think tanks are professors who have been expelled from the universities, theologians who have completed their studies in seminaries abroad, researchers who have been freed from prison, and scientists who have been trained in American and European universities and who have returned from exile. Together they produce hundreds of books, thousands of reports, and hundreds of thousands of statistics in their search for the knowledge that will enable them to understand Chile's present, explain its past, and foretell its future.

It is the first time that within a ferocious Latin American dictatorship citizens have had the intellectual energy to reflect upon themselves from within their own country and not from exile. Their reflections are almost always honest and sincere—and totally committed to the drama of Chile.

This is a unique phenomenon for Latin America, which can be explained in large measure by the cultural development of Chile prior to the military dictatorship and also by the support that Chilean democrats have received from universities and foundations in the United States and Europe. Their intellectual and financial collaboration appears to have no limits. The invitations from abroad to members of the Chilean think tanks to give lectures or to take part in seminars often interfere with the normal pace of work in the institutes.

The magnitude of the Chilean drama has deeply moved people in the democratic countries, particularly in Europe, where the ferocity of the military has reopened the wounds inflicted by Nazi savages.

Chile's political experience is atypical in Latin America. It was a pluralist society seeking a peaceful path to socialism, using democratic and constitutional means. The Chilean Communist Party always accepted this pluralism and rejected violence. Many Communists opposed the Kremlin line during episodes like the invasion of Czechoslovakia and differed with Moscow over assuring the security of Israel. The Catholic Church was also unorthodox. While it rejected the theology of liberation, it assumed progressive attitudes and joined in the struggle for democracy. Finally, the Christian Democratic Party in Chile was unusual in that it enjoyed strong working class support and included prominent trade union leaders.

Besides the academic and human interest shown by the outside world there are also some significant symbolic and deeply emotional factors at work. It appears that the world we still consider politically civilized sees Chile as a great contemporary challenge.

There is no doubt that all the research papers, analyses, studies, polls, statistics, and projects churned out by the think tanks explain and define Chilean reality. But they do not explain how to get rid of Pinochet. All the work has made it clear that there can be no solution to the crisis as long as Pinochet is in power. Everything indicates that Pinochet must go. But it is not at all clear who is going to remove him or how and with whom the succession and transition will be negotiated.

The researchers and the pollsters have demonstrated that, even after allowing a wide margin for error and prejudice, 85 percent of Chileans are ready to do something to get rid of Pinochet as soon as possible. But not a single study has defined a strategy that 85 percent of the population would accept, or a program that would be approved by common accord and thus avoid internal conflicts and divisions.

Not even the ablest researcher can replace the politicians and define the strategies and the methods that will unite Chilean society. So far ideological tendencies have effectively resisted being replaced by statistical data. Partisan interests have not given an inch, despite the magnitude of the crisis. But given the difficult conditions in Chile today, it seems too much to ask the Chilean people to suffer more dictatorship until 1989.

An alternative would be for the armed forces to select someone other than Pinochet as the sole candidate for the presidency. The military might be persuaded to appoint one of its own whose personality and past record would guarantee a peaceful path to national reconstruction. In turn, the political parties could promise to support and campaign for the armed forces' candidate. The president elected under this arrangement would be in power for eight years.

This option, however, goes against the interests of the Christian Democrats, who would like to impose one of their own leaders on the armed forces as the sole candidate for a coalition front formed by the military and non-Marxist parties. As part of the bargain, the president of the Christian Democratic Party would promise that no vengeance would be taken against the military and that no criminal charges would be brought against them. Under the pact, the democratic parties would be assured of access to all the social, political, and economic structures of society and would be allowed to dismantle the machinery of repression.

The Christian Democratic solution presupposes negotiations with the armed forces. It rules out the possibility that they might be toppled by force or that they might return to their barracks after losing their appetite for political power. It is possible that the democratic parties were bound to offer some concession before being in a position to propose negotiations to the military. But they would have no difficulty in agreeing to the exclusion of the Communist Party and the extreme left. The entire hard left excluded itself, anyway, when a sector of the right wing that had collaborated with the military regime was accepted into the coalition by the democratic parties.

A valid concession could have been the denunciation of left-wing terrorism and a public campaign against political violence. But it is almost impossible to take sides and denounce political terrorism while military terrorism continues against the civilian population and particularly while much of the violence is in the form of torture in the prisons.

Every day brings a new proposal or another original initiative. And each day the never-ending debate becomes more exhausting. Everything is debated in Chilean politics and everything is debatable.

One alternative is that the armed forces hold a plebiscite to reform the constitution. This opens up an array of subalternatives. The plebiscite could give voters the choice of reducing the new presidential term from eight years to four. This period could be looked upon as one of transition—under a military president but not, of course, Pinochet. The new rules of the game could allow the military to continue in power, but without repression. The constitutional reform could permit two candidates to run for the presidency—one representing the democratic non-Marxist parties and the other the armed forces. But the military know full well that their candidate would be defeated at the polls by a civilian. The suggestion of such certain political suicide immediately strengthens the junta's belief that Pinochet must be their candidate.

There is yet another subalternative. That is for the armed forces to authorize the reform of the constitution and agree to two civilian candidates, with the military having the decisive say in their selection. In this way, whoever won the election would be the military's candidate. This would avoid the problem of a possible electoral defeat for the armed forces. But the reality is that the candidate most likely to win, if two civilians contested the presidential race, would be the one who reached an agreement with the left wing, thus securing the 30 percent of the votes that this sector represents. The military, so prone to obsessions, cannot help but weave apocalyptic fantasies about the magnitude of the concessions that a moderate political candidate might have to make to secure the votes of the left to win the presidency. The political advisers of the military never tire of recalling that Charles de Gaulle in France, and Alcide de Gasperi, the Italian Christian Democrat premier, were both obliged to appoint Communists to their cabinets.

The military position remains firm. Any agreement with the politicians would be a leap in the dark. On the other hand, with Pinochet continuing in power, it would be possible to secure concessions that could ease any critical situation that might arise.

The military are also well aware that with Pinochet in power, even if he can be persuaded to make concessions, the situation will not become any easier. Just the opposite. Relations with the United States will get worse, particularly with Democratic majorities in both houses of Congress. With Pinochet it will also be impossible to normalize relations with the new democracies, Argentina, Peru, Uruguay, and Brazil, which share borders with Chile or are close neighbors. These new problems will have to be added to Chile's longer-standing diplomatic difficulties with Mexico, Venezuela, and Colombia.

The scholars know that their studies are read and analyzed by the armed forces. On more than one occasion, they have received requests for clarification or confirmation of data. But even over these matters of common interest their military counterparts do not make themselves available for discussion with civilian political experts. Among the young officers, the political equations are still very simple: Pinochet or chaos; Pinochet or the Communists; Pinochet or the "politicking" of the politicians. The ideas that fascism let loose in Latin America in the 1930s, predicting the decline of the West and the end of civilization, are still going strong in Chile.

The democratic parties maintain that their refusal to repudiate the extreme left publicly is an intelligent and even a subtle tactic. They argue that if the left-wing groups continue to support violence, their traditional constituency will abandon them for the democratic parties, as has occurred in Argentina. This transference of votes would be the beginning of the end for the extreme left in Chile. If the leaders of the extreme left ordered forsaking the use of political violence, the left would still be banned from participating in the next elections. Thus, the votes of their supporters would inevitably be transferred to those political parties that had refrained from attacking them publicly and which had not contributed to their isolation.

The military leaders, however, do not place any trust in subtle and intelligent tactics. They are still at the stage where they trust only throat-cutting and torture.

In any case, General Pinochet, who controls the entire apparatus of the state and a large part—how much, it is impossible to calculate—of the military structure, appears to have a different outlook when it comes to violence. He uses state terrorism to impose his power and consolidate his regime. The violence of the extreme left is useful to him in his plan to continue as president until 1997.

The extreme left could abandon violence of its own free will and to its political advantage, even though it would gain nothing immediate in return. This began to appear possible in the wake of the failure of its riskiest operation, the attempt on Pinochet's life, and the advent of a moderate leader in the

Kremlin. Mikhail Gorbachev, the new Soviet chief, has heard many Latin Americans, among them Argentine president Raúl Alfonsín, speak out in Moscow against the insurrectionary tactics of the Communists and the danger that they pose for the stability of the Latin American democracies.

The Chilean politicians have much to envy as they look about them. They have seen democracy return to Peru, Argentina, Brazil, and Uruguay. They also recall the Revolution of the Carnations in Portugal, when young army officers toppled the most enduring dictatorship in Europe. They remember the overthrow of the Greek colonels. Most recently, they have watched the triumph of Corazón Aquino in the Philippines, with the Catholic Church playing a major role. Chilean reality, unfortunately, seems to lie outside contemporary history. None of the examples of democracy triumphing over dictatorship in other countries appears applicable to the Chilean situation.

The politicians are also disconcerted and preoccupied by the changes that are taking place in Pinochet himself. While the repressive apparatus remains as ruthless as ever, his public image has been given a face-lift. A major source of pride for many years was Pinochet's knowledge that he was often compared with the Spanish dictator Francisco Franco. He copied Franco's strict observance of protocol, his rigid discipline, and his totalitarian vision of society. Lately, however, he has been modeling his popular image on Juan Perón, an Argentine, but also a general. With a dazzling smile like Perón's, perhaps Pinochet can maintain himself in power for the almost forty years that the unsmiling Francisco Franco ruled Spain. Or, perhaps, also like Franco, until death.

Pinochet's political advisers have counseled civilian clothes, spontaneous smiles, and improvised conversations with civilians. They have also mapped out a seemingly nonstop series of visits to the interior of the country, particularly to small towns where simple curiosity will guarantee attendance at the events he will preside over. It is in these country areas that fear, on the one hand, and scant interest in politics, on the other, combine to preclude any show of hostility toward the president.

In these small towns it is much easier to satisfy demands. Necessities are minimal. The people ask for subsidized jobs to tide them over difficult times. They ask for little things: a sewing machine for a family with many children; employment for an out-of-work schoolteacher; a public telephone; street lighting in one part of town; a few paved roads in another; a first-aid post; running water.

All his tours, all his appearances, all his gestures are transmitted by television so that Chileans throughout the country may receive the image he projects—of a vigorous grandfather, or somewhat elderly uncle, perhaps, but above all, of a very accessible man. The message is obvious: that a Pinochet-style government is preferable to the insecurity of democracy under the political parties.

In Chile the citizenry still remembers the total chaos that enveloped the country during Salvador Allende's last year. It is only a short step from the traumatic collective memory of those times to the shared conviction that it was that chaos, and only that chaos, that was responsible for the suffering that followed under the military regime. For someone as adept at political manipulation as Pinochet, that is a sufficient base for his frankly populist campaign aimed at winning the presidency in the 1989 elections. The 365 mayors whom Pinochet appointed in the principal towns provide him with three considerable advantages: they are all his personal friends; they are all military men, which reassures the armed forces who condemn demagogy only when it is employed by civilians; and they are all efficient functionaries.

The support of large and small landowners and of large and small businessmen tends to insure Pinochet's political stability. The thought of a return to chaos terrifies them. Even the situation of those living in abject poverty has improved, thanks to the crumbs the regime has recently thrown them. Pinochet has the funds and his 365 mayors have their instructions.

There is a dread that haunts opposition politicians. They fear that the 15 percent of the electorate the polls say would vote

for Pinochet would become 35 percent on the day of the plebiscite. The near-monopoly of the mass media, the manipulation of public employees, the unlimited funds available for his
candidacy, the terror, the provocation, the favors, and the
promises, repeated incessantly, that a transition to democracy
with Pinochet is far preferable to the continuation of the conflict between civilians and the military—these could produce
this 35 percent. It would be only natural for the entire population to conclude that if Pinochet had been designated the
sole candidate by the military junta, it was because he had the
support of the armed forces. At least, they would say to themselves, there will be stability with the armed forces' candidate. For now, at least, the political parties cannot come up
with a better offer to a population that is worn out, exhausted,
and terrified.

Even a 35 percent vote, of course, would constitute a defeat
for Pinochet. Yet it might still then be the case that no single
political party would have secured a larger proportion of the
vote. The result would not give Pinochet the constitutional
legitimacy to continue in power, but it could lay the ground-
work for a coup in the name of political pragmatism. This is
the kind of rationale the Latin American military have used so
often to their advantage.

If this should happen, Pinochet is then expected to switch
to another track in his plan to perpetuate himself in power.
The politicians call this Pinochet's "courses of negative action."
Nobody, however, dares to imagine what scope or character
his "negative action" would assume.

There is nothing more difficult for an opposition politician
in Latin America than to run an election campaign on volleys
of criticism and almost no promises. Latin American elector-
ates expect concrete promises that relate to their everyday
lives. They are not satisfied with theoretical explanations
about the benefits of democracy and the possibilities it could
offer.

As they are dragged to the plebiscite, the politicians are
drawn closer to a terrible dilemma. It has proved impossible,
despite many years of effort, to reach an agreement among the

different sectors of opinion on a convincing political project that could be proposed to the armed forces.

In the end, the politicians opted for a national campaign in favor of the reform of the constitution and the holding of free elections. Yet not even on such a minor strategy decision could the parties reach an agreement. They couldn't decide what message to send to the people, what the text should say, and who should sign the document. Finally, a group of Chileans without political influence took charge of the drafting and the signing of the message to the people. It did not jolt the dictatorship a bit.

The behavior of the sophisticated and cultured Chilean politicians is like that of a mad hen. Their words are the most beautiful ever uttered in behalf of democracy in Latin America. Their objectives respond to Chile's deepest needs. Their moral attitude is admirable. Their courage is moving. Their patriotism is above reproach. Their foreign support seems infinite. But none of it will convince the armed forces to get rid of Pinochet or persuade them to collaborate with the civilians in a joint effort to rebuild the country. The military continue to distrust the civilians. Of course, it may well be impossible to devise a political program that would appeal to the Chilean military.

Meanwhile the torture chambers continue to deal with those who take their opposition beyond the limits fixed by the regime. Yet it seems more and more unlikely that it will be possible to bring the regime to an end within these limits.

One of the political research institutes challenged the opposition parties to present, before March 1987, a proposal to the armed forces for their negotiated withdrawal from the government. The proposal was described as "a negotiated transition" and it was first circulated for study by the parties in September 1986. If it was not presented to the armed forces before March 1987, said the experts, it would be too late to make the proposal at all. Some parties could not agree on the measures suggested for the negotiated withdrawal, while others dragged their feet in the belief that the arrival of Pope John Paul II in April 1987 would create new conditions in the country. In any case, nobody went so far as to suggest that the armed forces would have budged even if the political parties had managed to get their act together.

The offer could have resulted in a renewal of Chilean political life. It might have wrenched Chilean politics out of its stagnation and helped the politicians to overcome their physical and moral exhaustion. It might have banished the ghosts. It might have got things moving again. Best of all, it might have made the politicians abandon the magic world in which they go on believing that what has happened could never happen. Least of all to them.

TESTIMONY

Chile has lessons not only for less developed countries. It has been experiencing in accelerated fashion the transition from traditionalism to modernity, from hierarchy to equality, and from elite rule to democracy that began in Europe at the end of the Middle Ages and has now spread throughout the globe. It has tried the formulas of right, center and left which have been developed since the French Revolution as secular religions, ideological responses to the new awareness of the capacity of man to use the state to transform society and achieve justice. Yet those responses differ in their choice of values to emphasize, and they can either organize society for change or immobilize it by creating deep divisions in the body politic. In the Chilean case, ideology divided the country into three groupings, and when any one comes to power the other two would combine to prevent it from governing.

(Paul E. Sigmund, *The Overthrow of Allende,* University of Pittsburgh Press, 1978)

6

While there are statistics in Chile that measure everything that can be measured, it has proved impossible to explain in figures what is meant by the term "cultural blackout." There has been growth in literature and art with themes of everyday life. But there is a scarcity of literature and art that probes below the surface in search of what is permanent. There is much artistic combativeness without creative depth. That, indeed, is what constitutes a cultural blackout.

Although there are statistics that provide alarming data about the economic situation, the cultural blackout may be even more serious for Chile. This feeling, however, is based on a state of mind that is fairly general but which has not been expressed in statistics, nor been analyzed.

It is known, for example, that in 1985 there was less output than in 1970 of essential economic products: steel, paper, and glass, for example. In 1985 the Chileans consumed 15 percent less than they did in 1970, although the 20 percent of the population that is in the upper income bracket consumed 30 percent more in 1985 than in 1970 and the 40 percent of the population that constitute Chile's poor consumed 50 percent less in 1985 than in 1970. Yes, 50 percent less.

It is also known that during the dictatorship there has been no artistic or literary work of significance. There has been no new generation of novelists, no new school of artists, no new groups of poets, no new theatrical developments.

Much has been written, painted, and dramatized about everyday life, whether about the shocking misery of the first years of the dictatorship, the collective corruption of the economic boom years, or the collapse of living standards after the boom. Each and every aspect of repression has been singled out and numerous intellectuals have led the struggle against resignation and the tendency to forget.

The denunciation has been direct, particularly in the alternative theater, and it has covered the broadest spectrum of intellectual activity. Yet here again the collective memory was activated to enrich the notion that everything in the past was better, both the recent as well as the distant past. It is as if Chilean culture under the dictatorship has possessed the strength only to confirm what everyone already knows and suffers. What is lacking are those three or four works that will reveal to Chileans what they do not know, that will bring them out of the anguished bewilderment of the years since 1973 and free them from the anxiety they suffer under the dictatorship. Most Chileans do not know why the tyranny took over, they have no idea where they are going, they do not know, nor do they understand, who is making martyrs of them, nor can they find any guidance from the confused signals of the political parties. Chileans need to understand how they fit into the human dimension—from which only death can separate them—of the macabre reality that they are living.

This is the moment when Chileans need a cultural work that they can draw upon as one does the Bible. To create this work, Chilean intellectuals must liberate themselves from their trap. At least some of them must break free. Haunted by their consciences, some Chilean intellectuals are drawn to a culture of denunciation or heroism. Haunted by exile, others resort to a culture of nostalgia. What is missing is the qualitative leap from dramatic actuality to the universal and human dimension that does not enslave them in ordinary, everyday events.

The classic tragedy—in the form of a novel, story, mural, opera, or work of the theater—does not appear in Chilean cultural creation, although tragedy is in sight of everyone, in the streets, as well as in the prisons. Yet all the suffering is made to seem banal. Chile is living a dramatic moment, but its drama has not been written. The lack of this drama expressed in intellectual creation is at the heart of Chile's cultural blackout.

Chilean culture refuses to recognize that reality is more terrible and, as a consequence, richer than the contemporary gallery of victims and heroes, and that the past is less desirable than the political terminology employed to recall it. Chilean intellectuals do not admit within the framework, desperate to be sure, of every creative act, the inability of the luminous Chile of yesterday to avert a total breakdown of its society. At the same time they accept that those who dominate Chile today are happy with the breakdown of society. The intellectuals are suffering from the one neurosis that is unacceptable in an artist: they are disguising what is going on around them before they have even tried to understand it.

It might be supposed that the debate between intellectuals and artists over nonpolitical art and political art would start up again. Nothing of the sort has happened. The debate concluded years ago with the failure of both points of view. No less than two generations of Latin American intellectuals have never once felt even a shade of doubt as to how much of ethics and of aesthetics a work of art should contain. It is now three decades since Latin Americans have showed concern about the right-wing infantilism of Jorge Luis Borges or the disciplined leftism of Pablo Neruda. Neither do Latin American intellectuals seem to worry very much, when the time comes to read them, that Gabriel García Márquez gives his support to the confused theoretical adventures of Fidel Castro, or that Mario Vargas Llosa wearies his days denouncing only Cuban and Soviet intervention in Latin America. Vargas Llosa emphasizes that he wants to see Latin America freed from all foreign influence, yet he omits to point out that U.S. troops are not only in Grenada, but also in El Salvador and Honduras, and that the United States maintains a mercenary army that has been unleashed, so far unsuccessfully, on Nicaragua.

Millions of readers in Latin America have the books of all

four authors on their shelves, but how many can say which of the four they think the better writer or which they prefer from a political point of view? The personalities of these writers lack the transcendence, from the cultural point of view, of their books.

Perhaps the cultural blackout in Chile is the result of the attempt of intellectuals to recover, many times at the risk of their own lives, a previous reality that can never be recovered. Or, perhaps, the problem arises because they are trying, always heroically, to change reality by sharing the suffering of their contemporaries. But in both cases they are so immersed in direct political discourse that only with difficulty can they elaborate an artistic discourse in which the words, the individuals, the memories, the fantasies, and the discoveries can be shaped with elements other than their direct observation of events.

Time and time again we come back to the same conclusion. The Chileans cannot yet measure the profundity of the breakdown in a kind of life that they loved and enjoyed. In their lamentation over what they have lost they can't admit that the life they lead today is the only life they can live today and that today is not something that is transitory. Their desperation is mainly caused by a political regime they cannot bear any longer. Their anguish is evidence of a human conflict, individual rather than collective, which, of course, will not abandon them, even after the fall of Pinochet.

Cultural creation has not yet examined itself in regard to the searing lament of a Chilean politician, Ricardo Lagos, who has returned from exile: ". . . the drama of a country that has seen emerge from its own entrails those who murder, torture, cut throats, and now even burn other human beings, and who brazenly walk the streets at our side, without our understanding where these people come from, or how it was possible that our society gave origin to this, to these thousands who seem to be normal beings. This is an element of moral crisis in a society, which must be treated with the seriousness it requires, not only by dealing with those who must be brought to justice, but, beyond that, by determining how a society could come to this."

The cultural blackout stems, perhaps, from the fact that intellectuals and artists felt themselves called upon to repudiate what was happening before they felt despair: that they decided upon total rejection in which the solitary individual adventure is more important than the comfort of collective sensibility.

Because they were alienated from a part of Chilean reality, the intellectuals converted themselves into partisans of another kind. It was nothing more than that. Yet they were in a country and in a situation in which the magnitude of the drama called for a compassion as intense and all-encompassing as was that of Dostoevski in the Russia of the czars. Or, perhaps, they needed the desperation of that small group of Jewish writers at the beginning of the century—Chaim Nachman Bialik, Joseph Chaim Brenner, S. Ansky, Mendele—whom the drama of the people of Eastern Europe buried more and more in loneliness and isolation: they sought visions before political answers and collective solidarity. And the visions appeared only in the most recondite and least likely corners of reality.

Finally, instead of fighting reality, the intellectuals could have deciphered it, even passively as Franz Kafka did with his own dull, boring monotony. Then, perhaps, they would have achieved the fabled encounter between the beauty of the past that they yearn for and the hateful present of the torturers. They might also have discovered that all this is happening in Chile and among Chileans. They would have been able to understand something about the myriad motives and the labyrinthian confusion of this sad historic moment. They might also have begun to have visions, and the Chilean people would have been given something more than statistics and sociological essays.

Chileans insist that they were defeated by the dictatorship but that they were not vanquished. If their intellectuals would realize that the Chile they believed in was defeated and was vanquished, then they could clarify their ideas and develop a vision of the future. Denunciation is merely a lament in the global field of culture. Activism is merely a form of consolation. The truth is the only way to prophesy what the future holds; but it is impossible to get to the truth if only a part of reality is accepted.

Kurt Tucholsky, a German writer who opposed the Nazis, committed suicide only a few days after sending a final letter to Arnold Zweig. The inevitability or even the possibility of suicide is something that no combatant will accept. But how much more important it is that in that letter, written in December 1935, two years after the Nazi regime came to power in Germany and four years before the Jewish Holocaust, Tucholsky was able to say to Zweig: "Who are you? A soldier of an army that has been defeated but not vanquished? No, Arnold Zweig, that is not the truth. Judaism has been vanquished, as it deserved to be vanquished and it is not true that Judaism has been fighting back for thousands of years. Precisely what is happening is that it is not fighting back."

That was a frank and painful prophecy that helped Jews understand what awaited them under the Nazis and it was made at a time when many Jewish leaders did not see any urgent need to leave Germany—the same leaders who, later, did not understand the need to fight back. Or, at least, they couldn't find the strength to do so. Of course, they had been defeated and vanquished from the very moment that they failed to grasp the truth of a Hitler who seemed to them such an improbability and, therefore, so marginal. Just like the Germans with Hitler, the Chileans cannot believe that the Pinochet regime is happening to them, the most politically developed country in Latin America. But many others did understand Tucholsky's prophecy.

It is a bitter fate to be lucid, said Kurt Tucholsky. The Chileans need such a lucid intellectual, who will tell them that the Chile they yearn for was not only defeated but vanquished forever, and that the future they must fight for has nothing to do with giving up one's life to recover the past.

Antonio Skármeta returned to Chile from thirteen years' exile in Germany. During his long uprooting, his work in prose and in the theater was an intense journey through Chilean themes. For example, *I Dreamed That the Snow Was Burning* describes the climate in Chile at a very special time: when the young workers were in rebellion in the 1970s. It is a description. In *Nothing Is Happening*, a Chilean adolescent is living in exile. It is another description. His most important, most successful, work is a short novel adapted as a play. *Burning Patience* is a moving exercise in nostalgia.

For the majority of Chileans, nostalgia is fixed on the poet Pablo Neruda. The adolescents read his love poems when they first were published. His face appears on posters. Portraits of him are everywhere. There is never a shortage of money in poverty-stricken Chile when it comes to buying his complete works, although his longer, more combative verses not only are bad poetry but verge on the ridiculous.

But there is much more in Neruda for Chileans to love. They love in the poet what they love in life. He was a convivial drinker. He felt tenderness for the sea. He made a cult of his meetings with friends and his houses were built to receive them. He was loyal, lovable, talkative, and unprejudiced. He embraced all the good causes—or what he thought were good causes—both big and small and at times broke with the rigidity of political discipline with a smile, although he observed it in his verses. He went his way, dissembling the Neruda of *Residence on Earth*, written over half a century ago and still the most profound and desperate approximation to contemporary man that Latin American literature has produced. He was also different from the Neruda of *Canto General*, that great literary encounter with the roots of Latin America, which was written forty years ago.

Burning Patience reveals the flesh-and-blood Neruda, not the literary creator. Neruda is the main character in the work, although it includes an element of contemporary Chile by showing the persecution of a young friend of the poet. But what was being celebrated by the public when the play was performed in Santiago by the New Group, under the patronage of the Swedish Embassy, in one of those small auditoriums of the alternative theater, was Neruda himself. The same thing is happening throughout Chile today. The young man who is persecuted by the police—he may have been tortured, or he may have disappeared—is not real. Neither are the military torturers. The repressed and the repressors are so obvious that they are hardly even stereotypes. There is no discovery or desperation in *Burning Patience*. There is merely a tender evocation to cling to, so that nostalgia may become a comforting refuge—for a few moments.

Skármeta himself senses in his work the constant need for protective nostalgia. Upon his return to Chile in March 1987, he declared: "The nostalgia that is in my work is not for the past, for the paradise lost, but for the future." But there can be no nostalgia for the future; there can only be prophecy. And there can be reliable prophecy only when the past is torn up, destroyed, and buried.

In Chile there is still too much delight taken in the past. The continuous celebration of Neruda as a personality is a pleasant fantasy. It is also rather moving but it does not cause intellectuals to plunge themselves, alone and desperate, into the nightmare world of reality. Yet it is only in nightmares, in that time and space in which nothing is obvious, that you can find the key to open the door to let in the light that will end the cultural blackout.

Writing in exile, Skármeta celebrated the Neruda that the poet himself liked to celebrate in the lost paradise. A word picture of Neruda as seen by Neruda appeared in the program of *Burning Patience:* "For my part I am, or I believe I am, strong-nosed, not much in the way of eyes, sparse hair on my head, swelling stomach, long legs, wide soles, yellow complexion, generous with love, bad at sums, confused with words, tender with my hands, slow-paced, a rustproof heart, an aficionado of stars, sea tides, tidal waves, admirer of beetles, a walker of sands, awkward in institutions, a Chilean forever, friend of my friends, mute with enemies, an intruder among birds, badly behaved at home, timid in drawing rooms, audacious in solitude, repentant without reason, a horrendous administrator, a traveling mouth, a drainer of inkwells, discreet among animals, lucky with storm clouds, an investigator of markets, brooding in libraries, melancholy in the mountains, tireless in forests, slow to answer, witty years afterwards, vulgar throughout the year, brilliant in my copy book, a monumental appetite, a tiger for sleep, serene when happy, an inspector of the night sky, invisible worker, persistently disorderly, courageous when need be, a coward without sin, sleepy on occasions, amiable with women, active when obliged to be, cursed to be a poet, and stupid as a dunce."

This celebration of Neruda makes the Chileans feel happy with themselves. This warm and spontaneous world must not be allowed to disappear. But the truth is that it has disappeared. So only writers who depreciate, hate, and flagellate themselves as an inevitable consequence of what they depreciate and hate in the society in which they live now, and in which they lived in the past, can break out of the hell of applause and celebration and help Chile to resign itself, for the time being, to living in purgatory.

There is almost no distance between nostalgia for the past and the madness of Miss Havisham, the abandoned bride in her tattered wedding dress in Dickens' *Great Expectations*. That is the case, at least, in Chile.

Juan Radrigán tried to use symbols. He is the leading Chilean dramatist of this decade and his play *Village of Bad Love* was performed at the Catholic University Theater in 1986. It is the twelfth play of his that has been staged in a period of only seven years. He has written a number of plays that have yet to be performed.

Village of Bad Love is a denunciation in which symbols are used to give universality to the drama. A group of inhabitants of a shantytown are persuaded to leave their homes with the promise that they will be given a decent place to live. But they have been duped and are doomed to become eternal vagrants. It is a work in which almost nothing happens. Words and ideas are the only means of expression, in place of images and movements. The characters are so lifeless that it is possible that all have died but have not yet been buried.

It is precisely because the play deals with a group of marginal people, whose presence not only the government but, perhaps, all Chile ignores, that the action of the play is plausible. The symbols do not have sufficient substance to show for themselves that the entire society is dead and that the drama that affects everyone—government and opposition, rich and poor, torturers and tortured—is that nobody has yet been buried. Everyone, not just the characters in the play, has died but has not been buried.

The two principal characters, Moses and David, the legislator and the warrior of ancient Jewish history, are the key to Chilean life as it is seen by its intellectuals. On one side are those who are fighting for dignity and justice, using peaceful means, however long the struggle may last and however miserable their lives in the desert will be. Yet Moses was considerably more than a passive legislator. In order to restore the dignity of his people he began by unleashing the ten plagues on Egypt.

The thesis the play proposes through the character David is that violence is the only way to obtain the land and housing his people need, even if all must die in an unequal battle. It is this thesis that triumphs in the play and it is also Juan Radrigán's choice. He said in an interview: "In the long run, history is full of these sacrifices and if words do not confront bullets, there can be no advance. It seems that the brutal sacrifice, which should not exist, is necessary."

In actual fact, when David confronted Goliath, he was the best shot with a sling of the era, and the sling was the most advanced weapon of war when fighting at a distance. That is not the relationship of force that exists today in Chile between the shanty dwellers and the bloodthirsty military apparatus of Pinochet.

Village of Bad Love repeats the denunciation, convokes heroism, and emphasizes sacrifice. It is as if the idea of abandoning this ritual, in order to plunge into sincere thought, is too shocking for the Chilean intellectuals to contemplate. Perhaps they are startled because they suspect, without actually working out what they think or without being conscious of it, that if they are to discover reality they must convert so many loves into a prolonged and exhausting hate.

There is only one survivor in the play: the poet who must save for posterity the knowledge of what happened and who must recount the heroism and the sacrifice. Radrigán says that many intellectuals have remained silent all these terrible years and have not protested. This symbol of responsibility represented by the character of the poet is a warning that the impunity the repression enjoys today will not last forever.

Heroism, dignity, sacrifice, and responsibility. It is a beautiful equation, distinct, clean, and honest. But it is repetitive and boring. There is much more in the Chilean drama. Its universality—which every cultural work aspires to—cannot be expressed in a pious proclamation of goodwill and warm sentiments.

Message and denunciation, nostalgia and description: the works of Skármeta and Radrigán avoid the admission of the profound defeat of the Chile they love so much. They lack the admission that the beings they speak for, and they themselves, have been vanquished. And that they deserve to be vanquished. Only when they come to terms with this fact will they be lucid enough to begin the discovery and the revelations that cultural renovation demands. Then these prohibited themes which, through history, many ideologues have termed, in the best of cases, unnecessary or, in the worst of cases, deviationist, will reappear in Chile.

In an interview of some eight thousand words published in *Partisan Review* in 1982, nine years after Pinochet seized power, José Donoso did not once mention the situation in Chile. There was no reference, no recollection, no commentary, no reflection. At the end of the interview, which was conducted by Ronald Christ, Donoso spoke about his future plans and the books he wanted to write. Again, with no mention of Chile.

Perhaps this prudence and caution has enabled Donoso to keep to himself or, at least, within his creative work, the first original reflection on contemporary Chile to appear in its literature. It is the idea that is developed in his novel *La Desesperanza* (Hopelessness), which appeared in 1986, Year 14 of the Pinochet regime.

This novel is the first recent cultural act by a Chilean that one can believe in. Donoso lifts the veil formed by the heroes and the villains, the martyrs and the murderers, to uncover the hidden life of Chileans. He reveals that even those who fight against the dictatorship may be cowards and antiheroes. And, most important, he shows that life is not all diaphanous courage in Chile today, that there is confusion and despair.

The central theme concerns a popular singer whose return from exile is a descent into a personal hell, and not a hell created solely by the military. The romanticism of the recently returned exile and the fixation with the Chile that has been lost have been exhausted as sources of inspiration. The banality of revolutionary dogma does not alleviate sadness; love is a misencounter and, barely, survival; then survival gives rise to feelings of guilt.

Contemporary Chile has produced two great singer-composers, perhaps the greatest in Latin America. Violeta Parra committed suicide in 1967. Victor Jara, held in the National Stadium after the fall of Allende, began to sing the anthem of Popular Unity, Allende's party, to raise the morale of the other prisoners. It was an act of heroism and of suicide. The military guards smashed his hands, those hands that had so often held a guitar, before they murdered him.

What would he sing today? Certainly he would call upon the people to fight. But perhaps he might also ask Chileans to immerse themselves in the hopelessness of the situation.

José Donoso's character cannot respond to this question. The fact that he not only does not try to answer it but does not even raise it makes him the first hero and antihero who carries his Chilean identity like all Chileans under Pinochet— seeking a place to survive, searching among the ruins for something as lost as love—even love that is tangential and confused.

It is a relief, finally, to read a work of Chilean literature in which none of the characters is above history or appears to dominate it. No individual act is more telling than the sad lives that Chileans have to lead. Perhaps the hopelessness in which the Chileans in Donoso's novel are submerged will cause other Chileans to ask themselves what there is in a country and in a life when no hope is left.

It could mark a more lucid approach to reality. It will be bitter, but lucid. A new approach could stem from a reflection on reality that was not subjected to stereotypes vociferated time and time again by Pinochet's ideologues or by those who oppose him. Donoso's Chileans have no monopoly on the truth, nor on anguish. They do not possess all the fear. The truths, so evident and so simple in the political proclamations, seem contradictory to Donoso's characters. The anguish is provoked not only by the destiny of the country and its people but also by the small destinies that are not to be confused nor identified with the nation and its people.

To feel that there is no hope seems to be a good beginning. José Donoso, a moderate man, is the author of a revolutionary book.

It can be said of *La Desesperanza* what Albert Camus said, half a century ago, of Ignazio Silone's *Bread and Wine*. An anti-Fascist exile returns to Mussolini's Italy, as Donoso's singer-composer returns to Pinochet's Chile.

Camus wrote:

"For a revolutionary work is not one that glorifies victories and conquests, but one that brings to light the Revolution's most painful conflicts. The more painful the conflicts, the greater their effect. The militant too quickly convinced is to the true revolutionary what the bigot is to the mystic. For the grandeur of a faith can be measured by the doubts it inspires. . . . On the other hand, there is no revolutionary work without artistic qualities. This may seem paradoxical. But I believe that if our time teaches us anything on this score, it is that a revolutionary art, if it is not to lapse into the basest form of expression, cannot do without artistic importance. There is no happy medium between vulgar propaganda and creative inspiration, between what Malraux calls 'the will to prove' and a work like *Man's Fate*."

TESTIMONY

Victor Opazo Cosio committed suicide in Caracas and was buried on October 30, 1985. The funeral was paid for by public charity and only an eleventh-hour intervention by a group of Chileans saved his remains from being buried in a communal grave. He died alone and in total solitude.

Victor Opazo, a cultured gentleman, professor of philosophy, director of public relations at the Quimantú Publishing house, a pilot, one of the first professionals to go to Cuba to help after the flight of Batista, a journalist and an outstanding intellectual, died in painful exile, condemned never to return to his native land. His home was a room in a modest hotel. He had been out of work for two years. His death became known only because a group of exiled Chilean journalists paid for a newspaper advertisement.

As the jurist Graciela Alvarez de Calvo said at his funeral, Victor died not only because he was in exile but also because of disunity and indifference. His truncated life must be added to the list of more than one hundred Chileans who have taken the decision to eliminate themselves rather than fall into the degradation that leads to absolute misery. This is a taboo subject that nobody dares talk about: How many men and women of all ages have committed suicide in exile?

(Extract from a letter that Virginia Vidal, a Chilean exile, sent from Caracas to the magazine *Análisis* of Santiago, Chile)

7

The Chileans have turned themselves into expert, imaginative jurists. Simply to survive they have to create daily strategies that will allow them to emerge unscathed from the twenty-one repressive laws that General Pinochet included in the constitution he got approved in 1980. The regime's laws allow its functionaries to arrest individuals without making charges, transfer people to other parts of Chile (internal exile), restrict personal liberty, expel citizens from the country, prohibit them from entering or leaving Chile, confine their freedom to travel within the country, discontinue the right to hold meetings, restrict freedom of the press, suspend freedom of information and freedom of opinion, suspend freedom to work, limit the right to form a professional association or a union, impose censorship on the mail and on communications, decree the requisition of assets and limits on property rights. Like a seesaw, when one restriction is unexpectedly lifted, another is suddenly imposed.

Nevertheless, however much time a Chilean may spend studying these juridical formulas with the help of lawyers who are experts in Pinochet's methods of repression, it is impossible for him to organize his days without being seized suddenly by panic. He can never hope to guess what interpretation will be given to these laws by the military if they arrest him or by the judges who would try him. That, of course, is in the best of cases: when he is taken from prison to a court of law.

The only alternative to living with panic is to try and sustain a minimum existence, reducing as much as possible the orbit in which he leads his life. Yet many Chileans are denied even this form of escape. Millions of poor people are condemned, by the mere fact of their existence, to be daily transgressors of legality as understood by the military mentality.

The Chilean military identify poverty with Marxism and are convinced that misery is an ideological choice. For a start, this means that everyone who is poor is also illegal. In any of the *poblaciones* (shantytown settlements) outside Santiago, four out of every five young persons are unemployed. They walk the few miles that separate them from the city early every morning. They beg, which makes them liable to be arrested for vagrancy. They work as street vendors, which lays them open to suspicion that they are selling contraband or stolen goods. They offer to wash cars, but members of the Chilean middle class like to do this themselves. In any case, they are looked upon as intruders in the prosperous neighborhoods and risk a night in a police cell if they are found "loitering" there. Prostitution is their best bet if they are very young, between thirteen and twenty-five, and are accepted by pimps who have good connections with the carabineros. They go from house to house offering to clean, cook, polish floors, mow the lawn, paint a wall, do repairs, wash clothes. They spend long days searching for such work, but few Chileans will let these miserable wraiths enter their homes. If they do get work, the pay is sometimes only a meal or cast-off clothing. In the early years of the regime, the police used to hunt down the poor in the streets. If they had long hair, or beards, they would be taken to the barber at the police barracks to have their hair and beards shorn. In the cities it is suspicious to sit down in a park and even more suspicious to be caught standing at a street corner talking or sharing a cigarette or a snack.

They can also remain at home, idling, but the carabineros

frequently raid the settlements and it is not easy for the poor to explain what they are doing there. If they say they are not doing anything they are immediately suspected of doing something. They can eat once a day at the soup kitchen, but the carabineros have said repeatedly and the official press and the radio and television have broadcast the charge that the soup kitchen is a Marxist invention. Any of these ignorant and meek people who dare to go to one of the soup kitchens organized by the Christian churches are warned that the church too is infiltrated by Marxists. They feel upset and humiliated. And they have no strength left. So they may not go back to the soup kitchens, but instead send their children.

They live in the *poblaciones* that have grown up around Santiago. Their homes are tiny, precarious shacks, built one against the other. It is difficult for them to get water, electric power, transport. The families have grown bigger, but their houses have not. The number of mattresses, or chairs, or plates, or cooking pots they own has not increased. So there are more people for each mattress, each chair, and each plate.

They know that when the carabineros carry out their searches, the troops will force their way into the houses pointed out to them by informers. They will break the furniture, slash open the mattresses with their bayonets, and smash the dishes against the walls. Anyone who has asked a neighbor to give food for the soup kitchen is marked. Anyone who has helped a priest or taken part in the church programs to fight drug addiction, alcoholism, or prostitution is marked. Those who were union activists or members of political parties have long since been eliminated. They were shot, have disappeared, or are rotting in jail. Now the danger lies in being identified with the church or with some project of neighborly solidarity.

At times it seems that the *poblaciones* are only sleeping and that one day they may wake up. During 1983, 1984, 1985, and early in 1986, the poor took part in mass demonstrations. They thought that Pinochet's downfall was near. They filled the wide avenues of the city and stood up to the assaults of the carabineros. Many of them were killed when they were driven back to the *poblaciones;* the bullets ripped through the flimsy walls of the shacks or smashed through the windows. But nothing changed. Pinochet did not fall. He appeared on television and spoke over the radio. And he smiled more frequently than before.

The carabineros killed, kidnapped, and destroyed. The miserable routine of everyday life continued. It remained as dangerous as ever to go to the soup kitchen or to visit the priest too often. Those who did were marked.

When the carabineros reached his *poblacion,* Benedicto Antonio Gallego Saval, twenty-one, quickly closed the door of his home and remained inside leaning against one of the walls of the room. A bullet pierced the door, went through his body, and was embedded in the wall. He died instantly. The carabineros like to use Uzi 9mm Parabellum submachine guns. The walls of the shanties cannot stand up to them.

Marcela Angelica Marchant Vidal, nine, was hit by a bullet while she was crying in the arms of her mother. A single bullet came through the wall and penetrated her head. She died in her mother's arms.

August is the rawest month of winter in Chile. Eliseo Pizarro was seated in front of a small fire in his tiny house. The bullet that came through the window hit him in the back with such force that his head was propelled forward into the embers of the fire. He felt nothing. The bullet killed him upon impact.

One of the tiny children of Lina Araya described what happened in a *poblacion* near Valparaíso, the port on Chile's central Pacific coast: "We were sitting on our beds, talking, when Mama fell to the floor. A bullet had hit her in the head. It entered her right temple. The bullet came through the window, smashing the glass. . . ."

The journalist Genaro Arriagada Herrera wrote about these shantytown settlements: "In 1983, with the protests, Chile rediscovered the part of its reality that, in the delirium of the economic miracle, it had forgotten. From the start of those mass demonstrations, names like La Pincoya, La José María Caro, Lo Hermida, La Victoria regained their Chilean citizenship and a place among the concerns of Chileans. Yet at the same time that the presence of this player in society was acknowledged, the official country discovered a way to negate it. A propaganda campaign was launched to present the poor as an unconscious instrument of violent conspiracy against the regime that was being manipulated from a distance by the political leaders. In this way the world of the dweller in the settlement passed from the sad state of nonexistence to being considered as an inert resource, exploited and manipulated by powerful forces of evil."

In fact, the *poblaciones* had been discovered much earlier by the Christian churches. The men and women in the church movements paid a very high price for finding them. The dictatorship tortured to death Father Miguel Woodward aboard the vessel *Lebu*, anchored in the bay of Valparaíso. The corpse of Father Juan Alsina appeared floating in the Mapocho River as it wended its way through the beautifully landscaped parks and tree-lined avenues of Santiago. There were thirteen bullets from a service rifle in his body. A Salesian priest, Father Gerardo Poblete, died under torture in the city of Iquique, in the north. Father Antonio Llidó, who was detained in Santiago, has been missing since 1974. In the first fourteen years of the dictatorship 106 priests and 32 nuns were expelled from Chile. Hundreds were arrested, interrogated, abused, spat upon, beaten, knocked over by jets from water cannon, and sent to isolated areas in the interior of the country. Insulting, threatening inscriptions appear on the walls of churches. The poorest churches are dynamited. A huge wooden cross, raised in memory of Sebastián Acevedo, the man who immolated himself in the city of Concepción, was sawed down at its base by the carabineros. Another huge cross, which was being carried at the head of a procession to the Hospital del Trabajador, was "arrested" and taken away in a police truck.

The most recent of the priests to die was André Jarlan. Like so many of the shanty dwellers, he was killed when a 9mm bullet fired from an Uzi smashed through the wooden wall of his house in La Victoria. Father André was seated at his table, in a worn-out chair which barely fitted between the table and the bed. The bullet burrowed into his head after piercing his neck at the nape. Father André, a forty-four-year-old Frenchman, fell on top of the Bible he was reading, open at the Hundred Twenty-ninth Psalm. Blood from his head seeped onto the page.

That night the carabineros had entered the *poblacion*. Father André was helping the wounded, taking them food and medicines and passing out candles. Because he had not been granted a residence permit, although he had been in Chile a year, he had taken refuge in his room. If the carabineros had found him in the street or in the church, he would most certainly have been expelled from the country. Psalm 129 in the Catholic Bible says: "Out of the depths I have cried to thee, O Lord; hear my voice. Let thy ears be attentive to the voice of my supplication. If thou, O Lord, wilt mark iniquities: Lord, who shall stand it. For with thee there is merciful forgiveness." In the margin Father André had written in his unmistakable hand: "Forgive them, Lord, for they know not what they do." They were the last words that he wrote in his life and, perhaps, represented his last thought. He died, in 1984, just like any other shanty dweller: from a 9mm bullet fired from a carabinero's Uzi during a nighttime house-to-house search. Two years later his friend Father Pierre Dubois, who worked with Father André in La Victoria and who found him dead, and the priests Jaime Lancelot and Daniel Carouette, who replaced him in the settlement, were expelled from Chile.

Every so often, an anonymous hand returns to rewrite the words that the wind and the rain or some carabinero on patrol has rubbed out from the walls of La Victoria. They appeared a few hours after Father André was killed: "The fallen grain of wheat bringeth forth much fruit." (The words are an abbreviated version of John 12:24: "Unless the grain of wheat falls into the ground and dies, it remains alone. But if it dies, it brings forth much fruit.") The teachings of the Apostle John were a consolation for the miserable inhabitants of La Victoria before resignation became their only resource. The words of St. John were also inscribed on the tomb of the murdered priest Juan

Alsina. Later, they appeared on the wall next to the spot where the carabineros doused with gasoline and then set fire to Rodrigo Rojas Denegri, nineteen, and Carmen Gloria Quintana, eighteen. The boy died; but the girl lived although 66 percent of her flesh was burned: "The fallen grain bringeth forth much fruit."

The middle class in the cities has also been pauperized, and the young people who have been forced to give up their studies for economic reasons and cannot find work fight over jobs they would once have scorned. The middle-class young who still have enough money to pay for short courses at one of the thousands of "institutes" that have sprung up are learning to type, to do rudimentary work with computers, interior decoration, handicrafts, and hairdressing. The girls want to be flight attendants or manicurists.

The poor, however, go on being poor. There is not much to choose between the bottom rung of their income ladder, which is begging, and the top rung, which is prostitution.

Playing the guitar and singing on the buses is a new form of employment. It is less dangerous on the buses than in the street, where you may fall afoul of a bad-tempered carabinero. You also have to select buses that are not too crowded because otherwise it is impossible to move down the aisle asking for coins. You also have to choose your songs with care. The driver of the bus will not appreciate protest songs—they might cause him to lose his license. Although the money collected does not amount to much, you stand a chance of being rewarded with a plum or a sandwich. The most successful singer on the buses is Sergio Gómez, author of "The Bus Polka." But it is unlikely that the censors will ever let him sing "The Bus Polka" on television.

The poor who live on the coast close to the Pacific ports can pick up the nuggets that fall off the trucks taking coal to the ships. They sell these in the market. They can also collect seaweed, which they offer to merchants who export it to Japan.

But most of the poor hang around the *poblaciones*. The bus from the shantytown of Peñalolén to the center of Santiago costs the equivalent of ten bread rolls. And you never know whether you'll find work. If you walk to the city you have to pass through a military neighborhood, where noncommissioned officers and their families live, unless you take a long roundabout route. The solid brick houses are guarded by carabineros. The neighborhood was built on a strategic spot, and it was designed like a fortress between Peñalolén and the city.

The poor use wood for warmth and to cook. To light their houses, they run clandestine cables from the power lines. Occasionally they come across an abandoned gas stove on a vacant lot. They mend it as best they can. Sometimes they can afford to buy a tube of gas for it. Every so often inspectors go through a settlement and destroy the illicit installations of the electric light thieves. Fines are imposed and meters are installed.

It is still possible to resist the temptation to embark on a life of crime, and it is also possible to maintain an appearance of normal family life. Children aged two to nine are accepted in the schools organized by the evangelical churches. They arrive in the morning without having had breakfast. They get their first meal of the day at school. Later they are given a midmorning snack and lunch. By the time the children are six, they know they must keep some of the food in their bags to take home to their families.

Parents are worried because drug addiction is spreading faster than alcoholism. A marijuana cigarette costs half the price of a bottle of wine. The carabineros do not repress drug-trafficking. Neither do they fight crime. The military commanders insist that all carabineros are needed to fight subversion.

Left on their own, only the shanty dwellers themselves can do anything to combat crime. But they can't do much. In the *poblaciones* an ancient honor code—you don't steal from the poor—has broken down. Vigilantes have been sighted. At night they go to the houses of the thieves and beat them up.

In tiny Peñalolén, which lies among the mountains, a public telephone has been installed, there is some running water, and some streets are lighted. But there has not been any news of the ten people from the town who have disappeared, and it is known that the three men who became political prisoners were tortured. Now, nobody remembers any political activity, although the most daring go occasionally to a church to record the names of the ten who have disappeared. Despite the fear, there was a meeting when Carmen Gloria Quintana was flown to Canada for treatment of her burns. There was a collection for her family. The sum of money raised is best described as symbolic.

There are no political slogans on the walls anymore, and it is possible that Pinochet would win the elections in Peñalolén if he provided a free medical clinic or a dentist, or even if films were shown on weekends.

Today there are three private doctors in Peñalolén. Each appointment costs two to three dollars. But medicines must be purchased separately in the pharmacy recommended by the doctor. If the patient has no money, then a few aspirins will have to do, even for bronchial pneumonia.

The progress that has occurred in Peñalolén may stem from the fact that the people once asked for some improvements. They were small requests—humble pleas, in fact—to the authorities. Anything more would have been dangerous heroism. Informers would have pointed out the agitators. Along with juvenile prostitution, being an informer is the occupation that brings most economic benefits. They are the only two professions in which there is no unemployment.

The unemployed spend hours sitting in their homes, re-reading old newspapers or magazines they have picked up somewhere. They listen to the radio or visit a neighbor with a television set. Or they look at each other, or at the wall, or into space. There is not much to say. Whatever happens, everything will stay the same. Life may get a little better or a little worse. But the difference between the two is almost imperceptible.

From Peñalolén you can see the city of Santiago in the distance, wrapped in smog. The air is better in Peñalolén, but that is all.

On September 11, 1983, General Pinochet celebrated ten years in office. He has held power longer than any other Chilean government in this century. Four days later, Genaro Arriagada Herrera wrote: "Upon the completion of its tenth year the regime finds itself in a political, economic, and social crisis and with a breakdown in public order. In the midst of an explosive situation, the dramatic failure . . ."

In the years since this diagnosis, the only thing that has failed for the inhabitants of the *poblaciones* is the prophecy implicit in the words of the journalist. The people don't believe that Pinochet is so weak that there is no hope of getting anything out of the government. Anything the opposition and the sociologists have promised them, and that they are still promising, is even more unlikely than the promises Pinochet has begun to circulate in preparation for the 1989 elections.

Pinochet does not fall, and it is possible that one Sunday a truck will arrive from the neighborhood where the carabineros live and that a screen will be set up so that the children can enjoy some cartoon films. That Sunday and, perhaps on following Sundays, free sweets will be distributed.

In Peñalolén there is an old couple who own but one pair of spectacles between them. If the church cannot obtain another, their only hope is that Pinochet will get them a second pair. That is what the Pinochet activists, who have just started to organize, are saying.

For these poor, vanquished people, the fear that the 22 percent of the lower class that is employed may be thrown out of work is much more terrifying than the repression and the carabineros' house-to-house searches. If ten or fifteen more people could find work, a new world would open for the inhabitants of Peñalolén.

Sunk in the deepest misery, hemmed in and repressed, mired in the hopelessness of the dirty, muddy roads of Peñalolén, with their disturbed family lives and their emotional troubles, a community can easily be bribed and corrupted by a dictatorship. All that is called for is a little more warmth and a little more food.

No people, so far, has managed to demonstrate that it is

incorruptible. Certainly no Chilean politician has ever shown that he can carry out the promises he has made to the poor.

TESTIMONY

I had wounds all over my body, I couldn't control my muscles and my body was in a permanent state of spasm and shivering. . . . My lips were totally destroyed, to the point that pieces of skin were hanging and I couldn't speak properly. . . . Captain Tellez shot off four shots from a revolver and then told me there were two shots left; he made me take the revolver and test the trigger by putting it to my forehead and made me squeeze the trigger every time I answered a question negatively. . . .

(Testimony of Alfredo Bruno Malbrich, presented by Americas Watch Committee, New York)

8

The streets of Santiago are clean and the sidewalks are washed. Like all capital cities in dictatorships, Santiago is part of the regime's image rather than the representative city of the nation. The avenues that were designed at the end of the last century, with an enormous number of trees, have been preserved. Some streets are like green tunnels. The newer neighborhoods of the bourgeoisie, which have been developed since the Second World War, and of the middle-class professionals still have old trees screening the elegant apartment buildings. The green of the foliage dominates the gray of the stone buildings and the red of the brick facades. Santiago has preserved its character—that of a city that has burst forth from nature.

The enrichment of the functionaries of the dictatorship, the high-ranking officers of the armed forces and the financial speculators, did not result in an orgy of uncontrolled construction. The regime built some new avenues and constructed a few bridges, but they were easily absorbed by Santiago. It is as if the city has maintained its character as its way of showing resistance.

The Chilean dictatorship did not carry out an activity that has generally been characteristic of dictatorships: it has not indulged in what Latin Americans call pharaonic works. In

Santiago there are none of the monumental structures that become perpetual testimonies to an epoch as well as definitive indicators of a destiny. Big public works projects have always provided a traditional way for dictatorships to employ their marginal inhabitants. The Pinochet regime has seven percent of Chile's labor force in what was announced as a program to fight unemployment. But the regime has not gone in for Mussolini-like public works. Wages range from twenty to forty dollars a month, a sum that barely covers the cost of transport if you cannot walk to work. The real objective of the plan to fight unemployment is to keep Santiago clean, swept, and washed, and its parks and plazas watered, and its walls looked after.

Consumerism was the great pharaonic work of Pinochet. He kept the country happy for almost ten years with color television sets from Hong Kong, dolls from Taiwan, automobiles from Japan, electronic games and computers from the United States. The entire world was happy to provide the no less happy Chileans with exotic fruits, English jams, French perfumes, hams from Spain, pasta from Italy, beverages, pens, and key rings. Indeed, perhaps the only pharaonic work was the invention in Chile of corruption by consumption. The energies of the majority of the population who rejected, although only passively, the dictatorship were spent on consumption. Meanwhile torture and murder was the response to the heroism of the few Chileans who were not seduced by Pinochet's creation.

The men and women of the middle class, who compose a large part of Santiago, had made the Chilean capital a city of balconies and flowers. In the dying hours of the night, in spring and summer, and often in the autumn, there would be silence and perfume. No city in the world was like Santiago for walking and talking with friends and breathing its air. The curfew emptied the streets of friends and it populated them with military men and civilians in unmarked cars whom the military allowed to act with impunity.

Yet, even by day, to walk through the parks that extend along the banks of the Mapocho, listening to the sound of this

narrow, swift river and lifting your eyes to the Andes, can remind that Santiago could welcome you like a lover—warm,
silent, understanding.

The exiles who return, having been authorized to do so by
the dictatorship, try to reconstruct the soul of Santiago. Those
who stayed in the city and lived under the stress of consumerism and repression have developed new gestures, speak
with new words, and no longer know how to look into the
deep of the night. But those who return seek in every corner
that other Santiago. Occasionally they find the old spirit in
some street, some house, some café, or in a particular group
of friends.

Perhaps Pinochet does not need pharaonic works that will
remind people of him in the future because he senses that his
eternity is himself. In August 1980, when it seemed impossible that the dictatorship had lasted as long as it had, a former
president, Eduardo Frei, who headed the Christian Democratic Party, told Chilean journalist Elizabeth Subercaseaux:
"Remember what I say: Pinochet will not give up power until
he is dead." Interminable years have passed and he has not
left, he is not dead.

Perhaps Pinochet has not changed the city because in some
mysterious way he has been captivated by the special quality
of Santiago, as the Nazis were moved by Paris.

It may be that the well-known miserliness of Pinochet was
stronger than his imperial instinct. He has constructed but
one pharaonic building—his presidential residence. Not even
Adolf Hitler, when he built his refuge at Berchtesgaden in the
Austrian mountains or his bunker in Berlin, could have imagined what would be accomplished almost half a century later
by someone imbued with the same spirit.

The presidential residence is a four-story building surrounded by 17 acres of gardens. The land area covers 20 acres,
with the building taking up 15,000 square feet. It is twenty
minutes from Santiago by a specially constructed motorway,
similar to the highway that Anastasio Somoza built for himself
in Nicaragua between Managua and his country home in Po-
chomil. The security system utilizes infrared rays and eighty

guards. There are three basements, designed to withstand a long siege. It is a genuine underground bunker. The garage can accommodate two hundred automobiles. The sports complex includes two tennis courts, an Olympic-sized swimming pool, and a multi-sports field which can be used as a heliport. The cost of construction has been estimated at between $10 million and $13 million.

The poor who are given work by the government keep the capital clean. You become accustomed to their "no existence" rather as if they were part of the garbage that they sweep up, the plants that they prune, and the grass that they water. They appear suddenly, springing into sight before you, when they need to beg.

Ten thousand people are given a meal each day in the five hundred soup kitchens that have been organized in Santiago. They are disguised as much as possible in order not to make the city ugly. But the keepers of Santiago have very strict working hours and they cannot afford to risk being fired for taking time off for a meal.

Among Santiago's middle class, 54.2 percent have a single course for lunch. Among the lower class, 73.6 have only one item for lunch. But the keepers of Santiago are in an even lower class. In many cases that one dish for lunch is the only meal they will enjoy for the whole day. Sometimes their one meal consists of only bread and tea. When they are paid, the first thing the street cleaners do is put aside enough money for bread and tea for the month. The children eat in the religious schools throughout the week while their mothers go to the soup kitchen. They try by every means possible to secure sugar for tea. A researcher for the work economy program of the Academy of Christian Humanism in Santiago, Berta Teitelboim, explains: "Tea with a little sugar, accompanied by bread, provides instant energy and fights hunger pangs rapidly and more or less cheaply. The people of the popular sectors consume a scant variety of products. We have calculated that the normal family shopping basket will contain no more than fifteen articles of basic necessities and that bread accounts for about 25 percent of the cost."

Pinochet has no reason to be ashamed of the capital. Visitors to the city agree that Santiago is clean and beautiful. Sometimes it becomes choked with tear gas, but only the center and the *poblaciones* are affected. Pinochet's guests are never bothered. In any case, in a couple of hours the gas disperses. The street cleaners do not have to work overtime. The problem largely affects young people, and only those who take part in the street demonstrations against the regime.

In the 1960s, the U.S. Embassy in Santiago, under a program for global assistance to underdeveloped and developing nations, presented the Chilean police with a manual on the repression of street demonstrations and the utilization of chemical agents. According to an investigation by the Chilean journalist María Luque, the instructions imparted in the manual are still in force. It is curious that the anonymous authors accept as causes of street riots the same motivations as the left. The pamphlet states: "A civil disturbance may occur when there is widespread unemployment. People become bitter and resentful and very often desperate because they lack the barest essentials of life."

The other curious thing is the scientific tone of the pamphlet. The writing is not hackneyed, and there are no stereotypical references to "professional agitators" or "Communist agents." It is not surprising, therefore, when the sober prose examines the problem to be dealt with in the most methodical way: "A group of people are to be looked upon as a (harmless) crowd until they offer resistance to the troops. Normally the first step to be taken in dispersing a mob is a show of force by the police. To achieve the proper psychological effect, it is important to make it clear that there is someone in charge and that he is prepared to act vigorously and that he has available, and is prepared to use, all the force that is necessary."

When all the necessary force is used, it means dozens of deaths and thousands of wounded, as was the case in the massive street demonstrations between 1983 and 1986. But in dealing with small demonstrations, generally made up of young workers and students, intermediate force is employed. Jets of water are aimed at the demonstrators from the Neptune trucks; wet skin makes the gases, which come next, more effective. The gases are also sprayed, from small armored police carriers called *zorrinos* (skunks).

According to the manual, the use of tear gas is the most humane way to disperse illegal meetings. The text goes into some detail on the effects of tear gas and gas that causes vomiting. The tear gas makes people cry and causes a slight itching of the skin. The gas that induces vomiting, says the pamphlet, results in "sneezing and coughing, followed by asphyxia and palpitations and, finally, nausea and uncontrollable vomiting and diarrhea. A lengthy exposure causes collapses and fainting and 24 to 72 hours is required for a full recovery."

The U.S. Embassy pamphlet is frank about the causes that may lead to a popular disturbance but not entirely honest about the effects on people when gases are used. Medical students, who generally organize the first-aid posts at demonstrations, have established that sufferers from asthma cannot get relief from their inhalers after being affected by gases. The medical students have also found that a large number of people suffer pains normally associated with tonsillitis, heart trouble, and colitis for several days after being gassed.

After the demonstration has been dispersed, it is as if nothing has happened. The carabineros themselves pick up the spent cartridges of the bullets—rubber or steel—that have been used, as well as any empty gas canisters. There are not many of these because the *zorrinos* are equipped with hoses to squirt the gas, similar to the water cannon on the sophisticated Neptune riot trucks.

9

Santiago looked clean and beautiful, although her old self with her hidden or lost soul was not for all to see. That did not matter to the twenty-one young, beautiful, and svelte members of the Dong Fang Ballet from the People's Republic of China. As they toured the city they encountered the same order that governs their own lives in Beijing.

Of the two major powers that were his most important friends, only China remains loyal to Pinochet. The United States is looking for an alternative to the dictator as a justification for its policy of opposition to left-wing dictatorships. But China has no objection to Pinochet. He may repress the Communist Party, but the party is pro-Soviet. And his fight against Marxism is no problem, because although trade is barred with the Soviet Union, it is not with China. Pinochet's hostility toward Cuba and Nicaragua is also of no concern, because neither country has sought China's protection.

The Dong Fang Ballet was greeted with curiosity and warmth by the people of Santiago. The dancers responded with a few words in Spanish. The ballet was in exotic contrast to the various human rights commissions that come to Chile from all over the world and are now part of a sad daily routine.

Pinochet parades Chile's friendly relations with China as a triumph of his geopolitical theories. In Santiago's Teatro California, the artists of the Dong Fang Ballet sang: "China and Chile, like brothers, long live China, long live Chile, the union of art and peace." They sang the same song in the cities of Talca, Concepción, Temuco, Chillán, Curicó and Rancagua. They learned the cueca, a popular Chilean folk dance, and sang and whistled it. They saw for themselves the peace that reigns throughout Chile. They were applauded everywhere they went. The newspapers tenderly reported on the Chinese ballet dancers each step of the way, just as they do when Pinochet tours the country. Their faces became familiar on every television screen.

The members of the Dong Fang Ballet saw for themselves that not only Santiago but all the cities in Chile they visited were clean, swept, and washed, with the grass in the plazas and the parks well tended.

Pinochet is good at finding distractions that support his frequent declarations about the permanent peace Chileans enjoy. The 1985 earthquake was appropriated by him in much the same way that Juan Perón used an earthquake in a province of Argentina in 1944 to launch his political campaign— the earthquake that, even more important, brought him together with his wife Evita. (Of course, Anastasio Somoza's regime in Nicaragua was destroyed by an earthquake, when the dictator was stupid enough to abscond with medicines supplied by worldwide efforts.) The earthquake was used by the government to co-opt all the energy generated by the sympathy that Chileans felt for the quake victims. Television, radio, and newspapers made a point of identifying Pinochet with the love that all Chileans feel for Chile and with the spontaneous mobilization of volunteers to help in the devastated areas. The campaign to identify Pinochet with the outpouring of sympathy for the victims was so successful that it was difficult to imagine such solidarity without him and his seemingly magical powers.

The regime has perfected the technique of identifying themes likely to capture the popular imagination and in using messages and images to distract the public. It has allowed *El Mercurio* to run up a government debt of roughly $100 million and thus is able to count upon the unconditional support of Chile's major newspaper. Pinochet does not inquire of the newspaper owners, the Edwards family, what they have done with the $100 million, and *El Mercurio* does not ask Pinochet what he has done with the seven hundred who have disappeared in Chile after being arrested by the military.

That is not the only question *El Mercurio* does not ask. But apart from not posing awkward questions, the newspaper knows how to devote large amounts of space to topics that delight Pinochet and also distract him—and public opinion— from graver matters.

El Mercurio, accompanied by television and radio, made a great sensation out of the wheat spider. The spider was discovered in Rancagua, some fifty miles south of Santiago. According to hundreds of reports published under huge headlines and announced by reverberating voices on television and radio, the spider was advancing on Santiago to wipe out its inhabitants. This ferocious creature had the entire population of the city on edge—alert, expectant, and worried. The coverage of its advance on Santiago was so intense that the humorous reassurances given by the president of the Chilean Medical Association, Dr. Juan Luis González, passed unnoticed. "Don't worry," said the doctor, "the spider will die when the song festival in Viña del Mar opens."

True enough. The arrival of singers from abroad and speculation about who would represent Chile at the festival provided a cheerful topic to replace the pseudo-scientific, phantasmagoric story of the spider. After the festival opened, there was not another word about the poisonous spider of Rancagua. Santiago was saved.

Pinochet's functionaries are not always so fortunate with their distractions. In spite of the servile assistance of *El Mercurio*, they failed to create a sensation with the apparition of the Virgin Mary, Mother of God, in the tiny village of Villa Alemana. The Chilean Catholic Church is not so easily taken in, and despite massive coverage in *El Mercurio*, the apparition was ignored and the story was dropped.

* * *

There are some things that the keepers of Santiago do not clean up. Nobody tells them what kinds of garbage to leave in the streets; they know without asking. The neighbors know too, as do all the residents of Santiago. A can of paint thrown against the wall of the house of a lawyer for one of the human rights organizations will remain where it fell. No one will pick it up. Sometimes a message is left, signed by the Chilean Anti-Communist Alliance or one of the other groups that are said to be composed of "ideologically motivated citizens," although everyone is aware that their members are carabineros or agents of CNI, the state intelligence service.

They don't throw just paint. They also drop off dead animals on the doorsteps of members of the opposition. Sometimes they leave a pig's head. Then the message is: "We are going to cut your throat." If the head of the animal contains a bullet hole, the message is that the recipient will be shot and the head of the victim will be sent to the family.

Within this culture of death, people who are threatened have developed a strategy in the precautions they take. Although an error in their calculations may lead to jail, torture, exile, or assassination, most of those who live with constant threats have worked out a way to deal with the problem.

Telephoned threats, say experienced Chileans, should be listened to, because you may recognize the voice, but you should never enter into a conversation or utter an opinion. It is difficult to convince adolescent children in a family under threat not to respond. They prefer to trade threat for threat and insult for insult.

When the telephoned threats are followed by dead animals or by messages painted on walls, it means that the family is on the brink of a more serious situation. It may not yet be time to go into exile, but it is wiser not to sleep in the same house every night. People facing this degree of threat are advised to listen constantly to radio news bulletins. If left-wing terrorists carry out a serious attack, there will certainly be reprisals. In the best of situations, this means imprisonment, but in many past cases people under threat have disappeared or have been found with a slashed throat. The attempt on the life of Pinochet in September 1986 by the Communist Party was the last major act of violence in Chile. But it could well be that the regime will do what it has done in the past and invent a provocative terrorist attack to justify reprisals and physically eliminate members of the opposition. There is also the continuing danger of left-wing terrorism, perhaps by a faction of the Socialist Party or of the Christian left—which have rejected the determination of the Communist Party and its allies to abandon violence as one of the ways to bring back democracy. The latter decision was announced in December 1986, but it has not lessened the tension felt by members of the democratic opposition. Because they have called for free elections, they know they are directly challenging Pinochet, who sees them as a more dangerous enemy than the left.

So those who live under threat must go on listening to the radio news bulletins. If there is a terrorist attack, regardless of whether it is genuine or an act planned by the regime, no time must be wasted in getting to a previously prepared refuge.

Even when there are no acts of violence to use as a pretext for cracking down on the opposition, every so often a democratic politician will find himself accused of illegal activity. Student leaders are particularly likely to be arrested on trumped-up charges. When this happens it is extremely important to avoid being arrested at night, particularly after the curfew. That is the time when there may be no witnesses and an "arrest" is easily converted into a kidnapping. Another tactic that may save a life is to insist that the commander of the patrol making the arrest identify himself.

If the police come during curfew hours, it is a good idea to call a fire brigade, pretending that the house is on fire. If the firemen arrive in time, they can be useful witnesses against the kidnappers—provided, of course, that a judge takes the case and decides to investigate.

Above all it is important to make as much noise as possible.

It is also useful for opposition leaders to maintain good connections with the foreign press, with the lawyers at the Vicarage of Solidarity, and with influential embassies. Their diplomats sometimes know in advance who is in danger.

The daily effort to overcome the tension caused by living constantly under threat, to avoid being arrested or kidnapped, to keep up with events is only part of the nightmare that opposition leaders must live with. They must also watch over their children, who are possible targets for reprisals. It is best to keep them out of politics and to keep them from being noticed as they go about their daily routine.

As well as creating a permanent state of anxiety, the threats disturb family life and mingle fears with affection. A solution, exile, is always close at hand; but it is never easy, even when a Chilean knows he should leave, to decide whether to send the children abroad on their own, whether only the parents—the visible political targets—need depart, or whether the entire family should get out.

There are financial considerations and negotiations with the United Nations High Commissioner for Refugees. This stage is usually followed by doubts and ambivalence. It is possible that Pinochet may last only another year. There are also risks about exile. The children may marry foreigners and may not want to return to Chile when the dictator is gone. There are grandparents, whose health may be frail. Additionally, going into exile means the loss of job, professional qualifications, and home. It is even more difficult to make a decision when the children do not want to leave Chile. When a family faces exile, all the countless elements that make up a life suddenly are swept up in a devastating whirlwind.

On top of all this, the rumors about the danger a person faces are always difficult to confirm and danger itself never seems imminent. And there are many moments when the regime appears to be crumbling.

The exiles who have returned to Chile cannot help those who must make a decision about whether to leave. The exile's return is painful despite the help of a team of psychologists sponsored by the Catholic, Lutheran, and Methodist churches. It is not easy to reenter Chilean life, and most exiles look upon the country as having lost its soul because political solidarity has been extinguished by the repression, and economic solidarity has been made impossible by hard times.

The crisis of identity suffered by adolescents and young people who return is expressed in their relationship with the country and with their parents. In Europe, the United States, and some Latin American nations, young Chileans have been able to enjoy and become accustomed to almost boundless freedom. Now they find themselves in a country that is almost unknown to them. They are startled by the constant warnings of their parents about the limits they must observe. In exile parents' influence was strong because children linked them to the reconquest of their country. The children of returned exiles look upon Chile, according to a book published by a group of psychologists, *Exile, 1978–1986,* as the "country that they heard about in bedtime stories. Where the grandparents, uncles and aunts and cousins were real personages and the geography, the mountains, the seas, the spring, were full of transmitted memories, of lost affections painfully recounted, of lost spaces and frustrated projects. It was the land of their parents and the friends of their parents, a land unknown, yet also desired, by the adolescents."

Once in Chile, however, the parents seem overcome by difficulties. Their spirits appear broken, they don't know how to handle the emotions aroused by their return, and they give the impression of being mawkishly weak, rather than emotionally strong. The children don't know Chile and begin to wonder if they know their own parents.

The stories told about the exiles are not encouraging for those debating whether to escape their dangerous lives in Chile. The psychologists warn in their book that, "without doubt, exile constitutes a situation of violence with a powerful potential for the destruction of the individual, the family and the social system."

Each day, more return and fewer leave, but the lottery of death continues. Each day Chileans brace themselves to face the psychological pressure of the threats, imagining how they will evade an attempted arrest or kidnapping.

Manuel Guerrero left Chile in 1977 for Sweden, under the auspices of the Inter-Governmental Committee for European Migration. He returned to Chile five years later. In an interview he said: "It was the moment of my reencounter with Chile, but it was with three Chiles. One is living on such a succulent salary that it recalls the last days of Pompeii. There is also the Chile that is trying to disguise its poverty by suffering in silence. Then there is the Chile of the majority, which is caught up in misery, hiding itself, but trying to sell a piece of chocolate, a comb or a mirror and which extends to the periphery where the young are sucked into the vacuum of drugs and precocious prostitution."

In March 1985, three years after his return, Manuel Guerrero was arrested in the doorway of a school, the Colegio Latinoamericano, in Santiago. He was supervising the arrival of the children for classes that morning. He was a teaching inspector. He was found the next day with his throat cut, at a deserted spot on the outskirts of Santiago. Two other Chileans, who had never been exiles, were lying dead with him. At that time Chile was under a state of siege, declared by the government to guarantee the security of the citizens.

Chileans are dubious about going into exile because they do not know what to expect. The exiles try to return although they do know what to expect. If they are opposition leaders, they face the threat of death. Those who are not marked politically realize that they face a long and traumatic period of readaptation. The psychologists note: "Upon their return they experience a process of regression which is linked to their encounter with a reality that has undergone important changes, and from which they have been separated for many years and which, as a consequence, presents them with the challenge of a new apprenticeship to learn how to deal with their changed circumstances."

They must learn how to cope with their changed circumstances while confronting the aggression of Pinochet and the silence and lack of solidarity of society as a whole.

After the tears of emotion have dried, after the embraces of homecoming are over, the family must look for work, a home, and a school for the children. It is difficult. Many times home is in the miserable marginal settlements, the school for the children is in a Methodist or Lutheran church, the job is in

Santiago, and the pay is twenty to forty dollars a month to clean the streets, wash the sidewalks, prune the shrubs, and water the grass in the parks.

Santiago is more beautiful than ever.

TESTIMONY

When you decide to be honest about your feelings, you spend the whole day in a state of fear.

(The Chilean actor Nissim Sharim in the magazine *Cosas*, of Santiago)

10

It may be difficult to believe, but never before in the history of Chile did the military have so much influence over a government as it had over the Allende regime. Moreover, this was not the result of a demand from the armed forces, as has so often been the case in Latin America, but was because of Salvador Allende's habit of appealing to the military each time he faced a crisis, whether social or political.

Certainly, Allende had no cause to suspect the military. For forty years they had played no part in Chilean politics, a miracle by Latin American standards. And even in September 1932, when there was a military intervention, it was brief and without consequences. When Allende assumed the presidency, there had been no Latin American–style military coups in Chile for more than a century.

Allende was not the outright winner in the 1970 elections. None of the three candidates gained a majority, but Allende had more votes than Arturo Alessandri, the Conservative, who was second, and Radomiro Tomic, the Christian Democrat, who was third. The unwritten tradition in Chile was that the candidate with the most votes would receive the support of the others when Congress designated the president.

During the electoral campaign the CIA was out to secure the defeat of Allende. In particular, the agency was trying to mobilize fascist groups within the armed forces. Before Congress convened, the CIA arranged the assassination of the chief of the army general staff, General René Schneider. Backed by the big U.S. multinationals that were operating in Chile—ITT, Kennecott Copper, Anaconda Copper—the CIA offered money to anyone who opposed Allende, be he civilian, military, or even ecclesiastical. The mass media and business groups were provided with ample funds for the purpose of defeating Allende at the polls, for arranging an agreement between the losing candidates to block Allende's designation by Congress, or, the last alternative, to prevent Allende from assuming the presidency after his approval by Congress.

Of all the sectors that took part in this vast, intense, imaginative, and in many respects repugnant operation, it was the armed forces that best resisted the pressure of the provocateurs and the conspirators. Their nonintervention was dictated by Chilean political tradition.

Of course, neither the conspirators nor the Nixon administration gave up when Allende was designated president.

From that time, such was the effort put into poisoning the political climate and so numerous were the efforts by so many different sectors of Chilean society to undermine the regime that Allende was able to govern for almost three years solely because the armed forces preferred to maintain their traditional independence from politics. There were many provocations and conspiracies inspired by the right and the center, but there were also grave crises originated by a left wing dazzled by its own slogans and unaware of its lack of power.

When the right reflects on the Allende years and draws up its balance sheet, it will refer to the administrative chaos, the strikes, even in the industries nationalized and administered by the left, and the occupation of land and factories by farmhands and workers. But the left-wing tally is much wider in scope: the terrorism promoted by the CIA; the campaigns in the mass media, financed by the United States; the artificial shortages created by industrialists and businessmen; and the paralyzing of Parliament through the continual sabotage carried out by the right-wing parties with the complicity of the Christian Democrats.

Allende deferred to the armed forces on many occasions, giving them the control of emergency zones, those regions where conflict had escalated to the point where the president had lost administrative control. He created territorial mini-governments under the military. He also appointed generals and admirals to his cabinet, put them in charge of supply systems that had broken down and at the head of disorganized state enterprises.

Neither the right nor the left can therefore explain the ferocity and savagery with which the armed forces began their government in September 1973. The genocidal fury of the military has no precedent in Chilean history and has not been explained in any of the studies of the armed forces that have been carried out over the past decade.

The overthrow of Allende had the support of important sectors of society. Given the armed forces' history of nonintervention in politics, the installation of a military government held no terrors. The military were expected to do no more than arrange a swift transition to a more organized and stable situation.

One of the publications most severely persecuted by Pinochet is the Jesuit magazine *Mensaje* (Message), whose editor is the priest Renato Hevia, himself a victim of the regime. None of the violent acts of the dictatorship has failed to evoke from *Mensaje* either severe criticism or a serious warning.

In the October 1973 issue of the magazine, one month after Allende's overthrow, a *Mensaje* editorial began: "No political solution was in sight. The dialogue between the Christian Democrats and the government had failed. The unions were on an indefinite strike. There was galloping inflation. The economic situation was catastrophic. The country was practically paralyzed. There was a serious breakdown in labor discipline. There was enormous administrative corruption. The Supreme Court and the Chamber [of Deputies] were questioning the legality of the government. The extremists were arming themselves more and more and had openly declared that the only solution possible was by violent means, at the same time that they were trying to divide the armed forces. The options were a coup, increasing anarchy, or civil war. That is how the military saw the situation. And, obviously, they chose the option that seemed to them to be the least painful."

This outline of the situation does not totally reflect what was going on. There was no administrative corruption in Allende's government. The questioning of the president's legitimacy by the Supreme Court and Congress was not part of the crisis—it was part of the conspiracy. But what was valid in the editorial is that it expressed the critical view that honest and democratic Chileans had of President Allende. It was also an indicator of the expectations that the military coup had aroused. The editorial added: "The road that the country has traveled under Allende, in regard to what is positive, is irreversible. There can be no going back on agrarian reform, on state ownership of the banks, businesses, and basic products of the country. The military junta has recognized as much."

There is an aspect of the Latin American extreme left that has been overlooked by scholars. It is the violent left. There has been too little analysis of its language and its psychology. Despite the impressive number of ideological papers that this fringe of the left wing has produced, what really gives society an idea about them is their language. And, surprisingly enough, the extreme left is delighted that this is so.

The very language they use persuades them that their guerrilla forces represent a real challenge to the military. Their psychological state induces a conviction that the military will collapse in the face of this image if it is accompanied by a few daring terrorist strikes.

This infantile thinking has caused disaster in three countries of the "southern cone" of South America. Such thinking does not explain—and certainly does not justify—the overthrow of civilian governments by the military. But it does provide an understanding of the dynamic that mobilized the military for a genocidal onslaught against their own people.

The terrorists of the extreme left in Uruguay (Tupamaros), in Argentina (Montoneros), and in Chile (MIR, the Movement of the Revolutionary Left) based their strategy on the achievement of one objective: to make themselves feared as an organically structured army and to appear as an alternative to the military. They realized this objective in the minds of the great majority of the officer corps in Uruguay, Chile, and Argentina. The intelligence services and the military commanders, to be sure, knew the truth about these phantom guerrilla armies. They nevertheless encouraged the belief that the phantom armies were real, so as to gain support for the conspiracy to stage a coup. In every Latin American coup officers with a vocation for politics play a major role. These officers are precisely those in the intelligence services and those who dominate the high commands. All the intelligence wings of the armed forces in Uruguay, Argentina, and Chile knew perfectly well that none of the guerrilla groups had the remotest possibility of constituting an alternative to the military.

So convinced were these terrorists who aspired to be guerrillas that their image was more important than organization, and even more important than training and supplies of arms, that in some cases they invented imaginary actions they asserted they had carried out. They also claimed responsibility for actions initiated by other groups. The Argentine Montoneros maintained that they had "executed" a police chief and his wife when, in fact, the two were murdered by the chief's rivals in the police force. They attacked a barracks, Monte Chingolo, even though they knew that the army was ready and waiting for them to strike. The result was an impressive massacre of civilians who were caught in the cross-fire.

The pseudo-guerrillas of the left in Uruguay, Chile, and Argentina had also convinced themselves—like a neurosis that feeds on itself—that they represented an immovable obstacle in the path of the military and that they would be able to prevent a coup. They did not avert the coup, they did not even delay it—nor did they provoke it. In all three countries there were other motives for the armed forces' taking power—the guerrillas merely provided another pretext. What the violent left did accomplish, however, was to grease the wheels of the killing machine. They wanted to cause panic in the armed forces in order to paralyze them, but the panic they created in the officer corps was just enough to set in motion the most awful killing machine that has been experienced in any of the three countries in the course of this century.

The inexplicable homicidal extremism that took hold among

the military in Uruguay, Chile, and Argentina is the other side of the coin to the declamatory extremism of the revolutionary left in those countries. The terrorist attacks never posed any danger to the existence of the state or the survival of the armed forces. The insistent declamation began with Commandante Ernesto Ché Guevara in Bolivia, when he forecast "many Vietnams" in Latin America. It reached its height with the blessing Juan Perón gave to the Argentine Montoneros. He made them believe that in every country there was more than one army and that the new army, the guerrilla army, would soon replace the professional armed services.

In general, a political force will always seek to magnify the danger posed by the enemy. It will try to demonstrate that there is not merely danger ahead but that the very existence of society is at stake. Hitler perfected this mechanism with the Jews; Stalin used it against the old Bolsheviks and the dissidents. In a way, although within the limitations set by a democratic society, Senator Joseph McCarthy tried to do the same in the United States.

Yet with the left-wing extremists in Uruguay, Chile, and Argentina exactly the opposite happened. They tried to make themselves appear more dangerous than they were. They boasted of their omnipotence, they exaggerated their operational capacity, they intellectualized their phobias, proclaiming a revolutionary military strategy. It was nothing more than a tale told by an idiot. But it was sufficient to motivate the armed forces, themselves victims of the manipulation of their own intelligence services, and it drove them to commit the first acts of genocide in this century in the three most civilized societies of Latin America: Uruguay, Chile, and Argentina.

In his conversations with the president of Syria in Damascus in mid-March of 1987, Jimmy Carter heard some reflections on one of the themes that, although he might not have known it, obsesses the democratic sectors of Chilean political life: When are violent actions against a bloody dictatorship justifiable?

Of course, in this conversation between Assad and Carter, which the former president of the United States related in *Time* magazine, there was no mention of Chile. Yet the theme is as relevant in Chile today as it is in the Middle East. The Syrian leader knows that his country is a safe haven for Arab terrorists. He also realizes that his ambition to be recognized as the principal Arab statesman in the region is undermined by his having made Syria a refuge for subversives. But apart from the context, and a number of misleading statements about his supposed ignorance of terrorist attacks carried out in Europe but planned in Damascus, Assad has worked out a precise rationale of violence. Terrorism, he argues, must not be confused with national liberation. Some examples of national liberation are the American Revolution against the English; the actions of Menachem Begin, also against the English when they were occupying Palestine prior to their departure in 1948; the Algerian struggle against France; the attacks by the pro-Syrian Amal on Israeli soldiers in southern Lebanon. Terrorism, on the other hand, consists of deliberate acts against noncombatants, like aircraft hijackings and the taking of civilian hostages.

In Chile, the debate is more than theoretical. Although left-wing terrorism has been condemned by all the democratic parties, it was more of an intellectual condemnation than a practical one. The condemnation wasn't credible because although the opposition did not evade the issue, it does not accept the ultimate consequences of its position—just as it has failed to do with other issues. The opposition will not explain why it has not organized a systematic and methodical campaign against left-wing terrorism, accusing the terrorists of being, in real terms, accomplices of Pinochet.

Much too late in the day, the Communist Party, the Christian left, and the left wing of the Socialist Party have abandoned insurrection and accepted, for the time being, the political route to bring the dictatorship to an end. Yet from their ranks sprang the militants of the Manuel Rodriguez Patriotic Front, which has claimed responsibility, in its communiqués, for acts of terrorism in Chile. A political trial should be held to judge this terrorist organization, and it should be the democratic opposition that takes the initiative.

A public campaign against left-wing terrorism would put an end to the ambiguity that the opposition is often accused of. Its democratic identity and its vocation for peace would be much more clearly defined in Chile. Opposition to Pinochet would also be much more efficient if a movement to oppose terrorism, similar to the group that denounces torture, was organized.

Here another element comes into the debate: state terrorism is not the same as terrorism against the state. The terrorist is a criminal because he operates outside the law, whereas the criminality of the state is not admissible. But when you live in a criminal state, and you reject its violence, you must use the same energy you apply to that rejection in the struggle against terrorist criminality. What other way is there for the opposition to dictatorship to propose the option of a peaceful political solution that would be credible to all sectors of the country, including the armed forces?

The magnitude of the crimes committed by Pinochet and the vileness of the torture have caused the democratic opposition to condemn the regime a thousand and one times. Yet it has never come up with a plan to counter left-wing terrorism. What is holding the opposition politicians back? Despite the accusations, the vast majority of Pinochet's victims have never participated in terrorist acts.

Some politicians—although only in private conversations—are prepared to admit that they will have to come to terms with this issue. They know, because they have it from the mouths of lawyers defending political prisoners, that condemnation of acts of terrorism does not mean overlooking human rights, which must always be defended and safeguarded. But the politicians believe that the youth of Chile would see a campaign against left-wing terrorism as a victory for Pinochet. Robin Hood continues to inflame the popular imagination in this corner of the Andes, so far from Sherwood Forest.

At the time when Jimmy Carter's article appeared in *Time*, Chile's left-wing terrorists were not disposed to reopen the ideological—or moral—debate on the issue. They had just seized and held for a short time a number of radio stations, as well as the office of the Associated Press in Santiago. There was no military objective. The only death, a cold-blooded killing, was that of a security policeman, a pensioned-off carabinero. At that time the political prisoners were on a hunger strike in an attempt to improve the appalling conditions in the jails of Chile.

If torture is the Achilles' heel of Pinochet, ambiguity is the weak point of the democratic opposition. The ambiguity can be seen most clearly in the opposition's approach to the problem of violence. It is perhaps understandable that the opposition has been able to do very little to eliminate the violence perpetrated by the dictatorship. But however little it has achieved is more than it has done to restrain violence from the left.

In March 1987 the Chilean Socialist leader Clodomiro Almeyda returned to the country after twelve years in exile, following on two years in jail. Throughout these years his faction of the Socialist Party claimed that the conditions for a popular insurrection existed in Chile and that guerrilla actions were the prelude to an uprising by the people. The Communist Party and the Christian left supported this policy. Upon his clandestine return to Chile, Almeyda surrendered himself to a judge and was absolved of the charges brought against him by the government: embezzlement of government funds when he was a minister in Salvador Allende's cabinet. The charges were so ludicrous that even the Chilean judiciary wasted no time in dismissing them. But immediately after he was freed by the judge, he was sent to internal exile in Chile Chico, a tiny village in the south, 1,400 miles from Santiago. It is almost like rereading *Christ Stopped at Eboli*. Pinochet has nothing to learn from Benito Mussolini.

Clodomiro Almeyda packed into his small suitcase a book, *The Name of the Rose*, by Umberto Eco. At last, he would have time to read it. He also took with him some loose pages of an essay he was writing: "Extremism, the Childish Sickness of Communism." It is the same title that Vladimir Ilich Lenin used at the beginning of this century for one of his pamphlets. It is possible that it will go better for Almeyda than it did for Lenin. It served the Russian revolutionary in the theoretical war he waged against the anarchists of his own time, but there was no way he could have foreseen the extreme left of today, which considers itself Leninist *and* terrorist, Marxist *and* Guevarist, and which is particularly widespread in Latin America. In any case, Almeyda's intention may be deduced from the title and from its predecessor.

And yet, his intention is nebulous to some degree. At this same time, Almeyda gave the following response in an interview published in *El Periodista* of Buenos Aires:

QUESTION: One of the problems that appear to impede even a minimal level of unity is the acceptance or rejection of armed struggle. What is your position on this point? REPLY: I believe in the popular mass struggle and I do not believe that a military defeat of the regime is possible, but that a political defeat is possible. On the other hand, I understand that the armed groups that are operating in Chile today do not look upon the armed struggle as the only way to topple Pinochet, and that is true for the Manuel Rodriguez Patriotic Front. It seems to me that these groups represent the crystallization of the revolt of the popular masses and their will to defend themselves against the repression that is suffocating them, and which does, indeed, employ violence and terrorism.

Chilean politicians cannot escape the ambiguity that arises from the contradiction between their intelligence and their sentiments, between reason and emotion. On the one hand, Almeyda does not believe that a military defeat of the regime is possible, a consideration that indicates his intelligence. On the other hand, he attempts to justify the action of armed groups by calling them the expression of the masses, a conclusion that is based solely on wishful thinking. In Chile, the armed groups are formed by a few elitists who are repudiated and rejected by the masses.

The fears of Chileans stem from different and numerous sources. And the repression has internalized itself in all of them, victims and those who are doing the victimizing. This explains why the majority have accommodated themselves to the situation. But there are other fears that are paralyzing: the lack of lucid political leadership on the part of the opposition and the existence of left-wing terrorism. It is an atypical fear, even under a dictatorship, and its parallel can be found only in the concentration camps. It is the sensation that the universe is paralyzed, that history is immobile, that what exists now will exist forever, that it will never change, and that it will continue in a context of violence.

Availing themselves of the pretext that they are practicing democratic pluralism, the opposition leaders discuss the best way out and negotiate solutions between the different currents of opinion. But Chileans sense that this is merely a way of avoiding the issue. Left-wing violence pretends to be an armed struggle. Yet Chileans know, almost through a sixth sense, that this "armed struggle" is really only elitist alienation. Both activisms offer apparent mobility and yet nothing moves. The immobility is another source of fear. It gives the impression that politics is waiting for the opportunity to break out of the vicious circle whereby left-wing terrorism provokes an act that will cause the government to impose new demonstrations of force. The terrorists believe that had the attempt to assassinate Pinochet been successful, they would have achieved this objective. They do not accept the possibility that with Pinochet assassinated, a new generation of military men would have been able to introduce a new version of dictatorship, much more prolonged and much more popular. It would most likely be a "socialized" dictatorship after the style of Perón in the 1940s and 1950s. For its part, left-wing terrorism is convinced that its actions will awake the sleeping courage, the slumbering heroism, of the Chilean people. The terrorists believe they will be the detonator of the "armed struggle" they dream about.

The one and the other are jointly successful in permeating with fear the daily lives of the 85 percent who are against Pinochet as well as of the 15 percent who support him.

To these fears others are added, accumulating together with the economic crisis, frustrated expectations, and unkept promises. The Chileans have reached the point where they assimilate change by overdoing it. The change promised by the military in September 1973 was converted into years of criminal excess.

When today the psychologists attend the victims of this criminal excess, after crossing the threshold of the conscience that is structured on nostalgia, they discover there is no nostalgia in the subconscious at all, merely a pathetic fear of what happened during the Allende years. One of the concerns they have discovered is the dread of change as a synonym of a return to the chaos of those years. The young Chilean author Eugenio Tironi has written that the terror detonated in people during the Allende administration derived from "the explosion of popular omnipotence" that occurred at the time. In describing the life of his young generation of Allende supporters—"we were gods"—he says: "If the assertion of a professor seemed questionable to us, we interrupted him without further ado and we refuted him; if inflation was too much and working conditions suddenly seemed intolerable, we would organize a meeting, a stoppage, a strike, a takeover . . . or we had the full right to do so; we took over the universities, the lycées, and even the private schools if we thought the teaching there was reactionary; if we didn't have anywhere to live, we appropriated a place with the virtual certainty that, after a time, we would be granted it legally; if the previously sacred hierarchy seemed to us not to be playing its part, we took over the cathedral of Santiago; if *Mercurio* was lying, then we proclaimed to the four winds that it lied; if the family seemed to us to be limiting and ordinary and even coercive, we abandoned it and in many cases we married—very young—taking advantage of all the possibilities that those years offered us."

The fear internalized in the Chilean psyche has two principal origins: Salvador Allende and Augusto Pinochet. The Chile of Allende was impossible; the Chile of Pinochet is insupportable. That impossibility, as with all frustrations that have a tragic end, has created a state of consolidated anguish. The Chile of today has put men and women in a state of barely contained panic.

It could be that only a rupture, or a long therapeutic accommodation with reality, will open the way to reconstruction.

Not the reconstruction of the country, as the government's proclamations have it, but of the Chileans themselves. The rupture that the politicians or the terrorists offer is impossible; the long accommodation that Pinochet proposes is insupportable.

Each alternative is like another turn of the screw.

TESTIMONY

My name is Mónica. I am 18. On July 26, 1984, the day of the communal strike in Pudahuel, I climbed a post to raise the Chilean flag. Shots rang out and the carabineros appeared. Four of them carried me brutally to police station number 26 in Pudahuel. They took me to a room where they undressed me, blindfolded me, and applied electric charges to my breasts, vagina, and ankles.

Then they all left, except for two who remained in the room. I was completely naked. One said to the other that he should not abuse me because I was losing menstrual fluid. He didn't care. He took me by the hands and threw me in a corner. I knew what he was going to do to me. I knew I was lost and so I said to myself: You have to relax and breathe deeply. This swine cannot hurt me physically. After sexually abusing me he began to shout hysterically. He said that I was a sickening woman, a disgraceful subversive. With my eyes bandaged I could do no more than kick at him. He began to squeeze my neck very tightly until the others came and took him away. But one of them stayed and after hitting me he sexually abused me.

After a time they took me away in a vehicle and we drove around a lot. They made me get down on my knees and they put the barrel of a gun against my forehead while they said to me: Would you prefer to die here or in combat? When the simulated executions ceased, I was taken to the police station at Cerro Navia. Later I was taken to other police stations until I arrived at the No. 1 police station at Santo Domingo. It was night. In the morning they took me to the Center for Feminine Orientation prison. Five days later they freed me for lack of evidence.

As time passed after my return to normal life, adapting to it became more and more difficult. Nightmares, anguish, lack of money, and loneliness made me decide to see a psychologist. He told me that I should cry, but I did not cry.

It all became complicated because my boyfriend did not know how to handle the problem. For me, what happened in the cell was terrible, but I saw it as being even more horrible when my boyfriend became excessively careful with me when we made love. I told him that I was all right and that I only had a few psychological problems. But he, with every gesture, every caress, every word, behaved as if he felt he was harming me. What this did was to recall for me every second of what I lived through in the police station. My relations since that moment have been black. I don't feel black myself, it's just that everything is black, black.

Deep down I realize the carabineros know that they can destroy a woman and that is what they wanted to do. They did not want to get information out of me, because they knew full well that I had done nothing. They wanted to terrify me, neutralize me. They did it so that I would never take part in anything and so that I would go everywhere crying. Once they pulled me off a bus. That caused problems with my parents. They were frightened. I felt abandoned. I lost my only two friends. My father got to the point where he asked me to leave home, he was so frightened. But I cannot leave him alone. He has no work and if I don't, who will bring money to the house?

I don't want them to feel sorry for me. What happened to me is not something to cry about. What has to be done is to work so that nobody else will ever have to go through what happened to me.

(Testimony given to the Human Rights Commission of Chile, published in the magazine *Análisis*, in Santiago, in November 1985)

11

Some 10,000 people cheered John Paul II and Augusto Pinochet when they appeared together on the balcony of Government House in Santiago. A few hours later, in La Bandera, one of the marginal settlements, 600,000 Chileans greeted the pope with delirium and shouted, "John Paul, our friend, take Pinochet away with you."

To these two Chiles, the head of the Roman Catholic Church preached reconciliation during a visit that for six days smothered Chile in dizzying words and whose result, quite definitely, was a disappointing misencounter. The majority of the country wanted to see the pope change Chile, convinced that he could do so. The pope wanted the Chileans to change, although he had no illusion about its happening after reading the reports sent to him by the Chilean bishops. Naturally, neither of the two things happened: Chile and the Chileans remained as John Paul II encountered them when he arrived on April 1, 1987, for a tour of Chile that lasted until April 6.

A year and a half of preparations for the pope's visit created an enormous misunderstanding. The misunderstanding resulted from the suffocating political situation in Chile. It was inevitable that, because they were so exhausted, Chileans would see the visit of the successor of St. Peter as the only way to displace reality. Not even the Communists attempted to minimize the importance that the divine presence could have in the search for a solution of the Chilean drama. The Communists fought for a place at the pope's meeting with Chilean political leaders and they fought for an opportunity to express their views to him.

The pope, unable to announce publicly to Chileans that divine intervention is not exercised in politics, kept within the limits that his religion has delineated for relations between God and Catholics. His addresses were no different from those he had given on his thirty-two world tours to other countries, but this time he did emphasize those words that could comfort the spirit even though they might not change reality.

The majority of Chileans hoped he would speak of free elections, but he talked of reconciliation. They wanted to hear a direct statement about the violation of human rights, but he discoursed on the dignity of man as a creation of God. He did not ask for work for the Chilean poor, but, yes, he was clear about the sanctity of labor. And he emphasized that the poor are those who are closest to the heart of Christ.

Only his dynamism and his stern personality averted the transformation of frustrated expectations into an agnostic rebellion. Yet those who manipulated expectations for eighteen months could not have imagined the spiritual fortitude of the Vicar of Christ, his theological clarity, his personal magnetism, and his sophisticated expression. John Paul destroyed his own image as a political superman, but he was not left hanging in midair. He clearly established the limitations of the Church in seeking a solution to Chile's problems, but he made it equally clear that he was deeply concerned with the drama developing in Chile. He was a magnificent witness who, in different ways and by various means, transcended his testimony.

The pope did not manage to make peace between the two sides as he had in 1978 when he averted a war between Argentina and Chile. He could not, during his visit of 118 hours, be a successful mediator between two Chiles as he had been between two enemy nations. Possibly he did not aspire to this. But perhaps he did make himself into something that the Chileans will begin to understand as his visit recedes in time. It was as if he held up a huge mirror to the Chileans so that they could see the image of a Chile divided, stagnant, and in decay. Chileans may begin to understand that the Vicar of Christ's only miracle was for them to discover after he had left them that only they can find a solution, and that this does not imply a total triumph of one faction over another. The sole workable miracle is to open a road that will allow the Chileans to escape from their magical world to the real one. A mirror can open the eyes of Chileans to reality.

The struggle between the two Chiles to win the voice of the pope had no victor. The battle to gain his ear and his heart was, however, won by the victims. That came about because of his role as a pastor and not as a participant in political infighting.

Carmen Gloria Quintana was able to say that she was burned by the military because the pope came up to her, of his own accord, and embraced her. He took her disfigured face in his hands. Now the military commanders realize that the Vicar of Christ knows what they did to her.

The papal nuncio, Monsignor Angelo Sodano, avoided any mention of the name of André Jarlan when his Bible, bloodstained because the priest's head fell on its pages after he was killed by a police bullet, was given to the pope. But the Vicar of Christ heard the name of the martyred priest proclaimed by 600,000 throats during his meeting with the poor. He received the Bible of Father André from the settlers of La Victoria.

At this same meeting, the nuncio, Monsignor Angelo Sodano, and the conservative sector of the Church could not close the eyes nor cover the ears of the pope. He heard Luisa Riveros, an inhabitant of a *poblacion*, say: "We are mothers, who give life and care for life. We do not want violence. That is why we are with those who are victims and with their families. We settlers do not want to see anyone killed, not civilians, not men in uniform. We want a decent life for everyone.

Without dictatorship. That is why we visit the political prisoners and those who have been tortured. We ask for justice and the return of those who have been exiled. We are with the families of the detainees who have disappeared and we want to be listened to and respected. At this moment, there are fourteen political prisoners whose lives are in danger."

The nuncio had made Luisa Riveros present various drafts of her address to him, all edited by him. But she managed to introduce, without previously informing the nuncio, the issues of torture, the political prisoners, and the disappeared. When she concluded her three-minute address, John Paul embraced her, and Luisa Riveros was able to whisper in his ear: "Our people are bleeding with pain, because the streets are flowing with blood . . . because the young people want justice." The pope hugged her closer to him and assured her, in a low voice, "Everything passes."

The Holy Father did not bring down Pinochet. It is a pity that so many Chileans had waited with such anxiety and had imagined with such fervor that this could have occurred. After the pope's departure, when they were calmer and could reflect on his visit, Chileans discovered that the Vicar of Christ had demolished the wall of silence that the government had tried to build around his visit. The two occasions when the pope clearly and publicly showed his emotion and grief were when he embraced Carmen Gloria Quintana and when he listened to Luisa Riveros. The burned girl arrived by air from Canada, thanks to the generosity of thousands of Canadians. Luisa Riveros came on foot from the distant marginal settlement where she lives and walked back to the shack she calls home. Now Pinochet cannot deny, although he may pretend to ignore it, the message that those two Chilean women proclaimed *urbi et orbi*.

The government called the pope a Messenger of Peace. The majority of Chileans called him Messenger of Life. The church officially named him "Messenger of Life and Pilgrim of Peace." The government invested all its energy in transmitting the image of the Vicar of Christ standing next to the dictator of Chile on the balcony of Government House. Chileans, however, selected the image of the pope taking the head of the burned girl in his hands and resting his cheek on the scarred face of Carmen Gloria Quintana. The government unfurled the banner of peace that it says reigns in Chile, interpreting peace to mean the conservation of the status quo and the passive acceptance by the population of the government's plans for the future. Most Chileans interpreted the message of the Vicar of Christ as a convocation to life: open the jails; declare an end to exile; let us decide our present. The government placed all its bets on emphasizing the defeat the regime had inflicted on Marxism, perhaps unaware that the pope has good relations with the Italian Communist Party. The government may also have been unaware that the Church's opposition to Marxism does not extend to cutting the throats of Communists, the practice Pinochet prefers. If the pope's attitude to communism needed to be expressed with a symbol for the Chileans, they now realize that the Marxist leaders were invited to the meeting between the politicians and the pope because of an express instruction from the Vatican.

The government and the official media did not report the statements made by the pope to the journalists who accompanied him on the flight from Rome. He said: "Certainly in Chile we are going to encounter a system that is at this moment dictatorial. But this system by its own definition is transitory. Dictatorships are one thing and dictators are another. The dictator must pass. The return to democracy is therefore guaranteed. A dictatorship as a continuous system is another thing entirely." John Paul was referring to the regime in Poland when he mentioned dictatorship as a system, but when he was asked if the Chilean regime would pass, he said: "That is what I believe. At least, that is what the experience in Latin America shows."

Pinochet's government concluded that these ideas were expressed merely for the consumption of a European audience, or that they had been extracted from him by journalists, because they were not repeated during his visit. The regime saw this as a triumph. Yet even though the official press did not report the instructions that the pope gave to the Chilean bishops during the meeting of the episcopal conference, there is now little room for discussion between conservative and progressive priests about the role of the church in politics. John Paul told the bishops: "It is necessary, as Vatican Council II pointed out, that within every country there be effective possibilities for taking part, freely and actively, in establishing the juridical foundations of the political community, in the government and in public affairs, in the determination of the fields of action, in deciding the limits of the different institutions, and in the election of those who govern."

Despite the fact that he is a leader of religion, the pope converted his visit into a thunderclap of realism. The Chileans called him Hurricane Wojtyla. Thanks to the hurricane it is now clear that there is no magic in politics, that there are no made-to-measure miracles for desperate people. Nevertheless, as they listened to the pope, watching his gestures, his smiles, his hands, and his expressions, analyzing the speeches he gave and those that he listened to, Chileans could not resist the temptation to create another fantasy. They had, or believed they had, an ultimate reason to dream: the forty-two minutes in Government House that the pope and the dictator were alone together. Nothing is known about their conversation. But something is evident: it was the only part of the pope's visit that Pinochet did not dare to try to manipulate by means of his control over the mass media. Had the general made any false claim about what the two men talked about when they were alone, a denial from the pope would have fallen on Pinochet's head like the scourge of God.

John Paul II was told, before his journey, that Paul VI did not hide his indignation over what happened in Chile in September 1973. His predecessor had spoken clearly of "the tragic political drama of Chile" after Pinochet had overthrown Salvador Allende. He referred publicly to "the violent repressions" and only a gesture of the then primate of Chile averted an open condemnation of the coup. Cardinal Raúl Silva Henríquez believed that by using his good offices with the pope he would be able to influence the military junta for the good.

So, inspired by the cardinal, the episcopate issued a prudent statement in 1973: "It pains us immensely, and it depresses us, that our streets, our settlements, and our factories have been dyed red with blood and flow with the tears of so many women and children. We ask respect for those who have fallen in the struggle and, in the first place, for him who until Tuesday September 11 was president of the republic."

It did not take long for Raúl Silva Henríquez and the bishops to realize the magnitude of their error. They verified, with shock and sorrow, that although all the military officers are Catholics who attend mass, confess to their priests, and baptize their children in the church, cannibalism had been germinating in the spirit of these men. The church had preached the gospel, had given them communion, but it had all been in vain. The church decided that it was necessary to create a special committee to be called Cooperation for Peace in Chile, which in 1976 became the Vicariate of Solidarity.

General Pinochet wrote of this institution on November 11, 1975, in a letter to the archbishop: "The organism in question is a means by which the Marxist-Leninists create problems that disturb the quiet and tranquillity which is necessary for the citizens."

Pinochet realized that he had encountered his most formidable enemy: an impressive juridical organization set up with the full spiritual support of the church to defend the victims of the regime.

If John Paul had granted Pinochet one wish, there can be no doubt he would have chosen the suppression of the Vicariate of Solidarity. In its shabby offices, which are integrated into the cathedral in Santiago, the Vicariate records human rights violations that take place in Chile. It defends every political prisoner who has not employed violence in the struggle against the dictatorship, following an investigation by the Vicariate's lawyers, because the government's accusations, usually false, are not accepted.

In a survey carried out toward the middle of 1984 by the Center for the Study of Contemporary Reality in Santiago to measure the amount of support that the population gives to various institutions, the Catholic Church came in first. Immediately following it in public approval was the Vicariate of Solidarity. On a scale of 1 to 7, both the Catholic Church and the Vicariate of Solidarity were given a grade of 5.7. In third place was the Federation of Students with 5.1. The government's grade was 3.6.

It is surprising that a human rights organization should be so widely known in a country with a population so spread out as in narrow, elongated Chile. It was not surprising that John Paul gave his full support to the Vicariate of Solidarity, the government's worst nightmare. He visited the offices, he met the staff, and he called upon them to continue their work, emphasizing that the Gospel consistently urges respect for human rights.

El Mercurio made a point of emphasizing that the Vicar of Christ had not come to Chile to concern himself with democracy. The newspaper recalled a phrase used by John Paul during his conversation with journalists on the flight from Rome: "I am not an evangelist of democracy, but an evangelist of the message of Christ." But the pope's evangelism, which the government tried to use to win over John Paul, was the reason he went to the Vicariate of Solidarity. And it was his evangelism that enabled the human rights workers to hear from the pope himself just how deeply imbued in Christianity is the struggle for human rights.

The days are long past when the principal problem of the Vicariate of Solidarity was to discover the whereabouts of people taken prisoner by the regime. At police stations and barracks, officers would deny they were holding prisoners. In those days, when human rights lawyers identified a clandestine prison, they would knock in vain on the door. Then, after a long time, a peephole began to open in the door. Then the holes opened wider, then the cell doors, then the anonymous graves.

Although the Vicariate of Solidarity has only fifteen full-time lawyers, thanks to international aid they are surrounded by computers and the most modern equipment. When there is an emergency they consult with the experts at the Chilean

Human Rights Commission. When they need to compare international legislation or to make information widely available outside Chile, they use the resources of Americas Watch in New York and Amnesty International in London. When they have a need for shelter or escape, or seek special information through confidential channels, there are the diplomatic missions in Santiago that act as watchdogs over the regime—the embassies of France, Italy, Canada, West Germany, Sweden, Spain, the United States, Argentina, and Holland.

The lawyers of the Vicariate of Solidarity estimate that each case calls for three weeks of intensive work, but this does not include attending to the families of political prisoners. Many families are paralyzed by fear, especially people from rural areas, and they tend to think they must abandon someone who has become a political prisoner simply in order to save the other members of the family. The lawyers must explain the intricacies of the law in order to get approval to represent an imprisoned relative before the courts. This is particularly important in the case of detainees who have disappeared. The Vicariate of Solidarity also provides psychological support and therapy to help families deal with the emotional problems that arise.

Reports on violations of human rights reach the Vicariate of Solidarity from every corner of Chile. The reports range from an anonymous telephone threat to a priest who helps the poor, to the breaking of windows in a rural village where the population has expressed its desire for democracy and legality. Another report begins by describing the insults that a woman received when she visited her son in prison and goes on to outline in detail the torture inflicted on him. Other documents tell of the whereabouts of prisoners who have been moved from prison so that they can be tortured in locations that cannot easily be identified. Then there are the grisly discoveries, like the collective graves in Lonquén, where the bones of prisoners who disappeared more than ten years ago have been found.

Everything is recorded in the Vicariate of Solidarity, and then the information is published throughout the country and abroad. Reports go to the international human rights organizations, but they are also transmitted to tiny parishes dispersed throughout Chile, so that they may be read at Sunday mass.

No crime has been disguised, disproved, or hidden by the regime, thanks to this vigilance. Each regulation of the dictatorship is analyzed by the human rights lawyers. They dissect the juridical structure of the government's dictates and inform the United Nations human rights commission if they violate international treaties signed by Chile.

This remarkable task has made the Vicariate of Solidarity the conscience, alive and alert, of Chile. It was shocking, but not surprising, when the director of the organization's archives, José Manuel Parada, a thirty-four-year-old sociologist, was fingered by the dictatorship. He was kidnapped, his throat cut, and his body dumped in a field in March 1985. He had been working with the church on human rights for twelve years. Throughout the world, men and women involved in human rights organizations knew of José Manuel Parada. They could trust his information about what was going on in Chile. And his credibility was much greater than that of Pinochet.

Enrique Palet, executive secretary of the Vicariate of Solidarity, expressed horror when the news broke: "In the name of God, we say: this is not just, this is not human, this is not Christian."

Two years after José Manuel Parada bled to death, the Vicar of Christ arrived in Santiago and affirmed as he stood before the men and women of the Vicariate of Solidarity, before those who are still alive, that they, by their actions, are the true Christians of Chile.

Pinochet will never forget those words.

TESTIMONY

Woe to them that make wicked laws,
and when they write, write injustices,
to oppress the poor in judgment,
and do violence to the cause
of the humble of my people,
that widows might be their prey,
and that they might rob the fatherless!

What will you do in the day of visitation,
and of the calamity which cometh from afar?
   To whom will you flee for help?
And where will you leave your glory . . . ?

Isaiah 10:1–3

(Included in an "Open Letter to Pinochet" from the Christian Confraternity of Churches, Santiago, Chile, August 29, 1986)

12

In October 1974, in Suresnes, France, those attending the congress of the Spanish Socialist Party were surprised by the intervention of a thirty-two-year-old man who used the name Isidoro for his undercover work in the resistance against Franco. Facing the veterans of the civil war and the historic glories of the Republican resistance—Isidoro had been born thirteen years after the triumph of Francisco Franco—he called for a revision of the methods used in the struggle against the dictatorship. Actually he was trying to change the concept of the political struggle of Spanish socialism. For Isidoro, there was no nostalgia for the old days of the Republic. He had known only the Spain of Franco. He could not allow himself fantasies about military actions: he lived in Spain. The everyday reality of Spain, as well as the Fascist textbooks that he had been obliged to study at school and at the university, was very clear: the heroic Spanish Republic had been defeated, definitively. It was obvious that it was necessary to think of something else, something that was possible in Franco's Spain, not the Spain imagined by the exiled Republicans in France.

The venerable leader Rodolfo Llopis was not successful in getting himself reelected secretary-general of the Spanish Socialist Party. The congress backed young Isidoro, and now the party would have a new secretary-general, who lived in Spain.

Isidoro sought a democracy of the future, not a republic of the past. He did not believe that it was possible to overthrow Franco, nor did he subscribe to the need for violence. He did not think it was absolutely necessary to restore the republic, nor did he believe that the idea of a monarchy, which had just been proposed, was unacceptable. What the young secretary-general did feel was that reaching peace with Spain did not mean reaching peace with Franco. He also thought that preparations had to be made for a future democracy.

The "Isidoro" who surprised the veterans at the congress in Suresnes is the present prime minister of Spain, Felipe González.

What is amazing in Chile is that the politicians of the democratic opposition still believe that they can make plans for their struggle for democracy while ignoring the existence of Pinochet and his power. Their obsession with finding an answer to the question of Pinochet's fate has prevented them from thinking about the future of Chile. They have assumed so often that they could bring the regime to an end that it is now difficult for them to accept the fact that they have to operate within the regime. They have to find a road to democracy within an antidemocratic context.

Yet even in this context the democratic opposition can count on something that Isidoro would certainly have enjoyed: four major weekly magazines and two morning newspapers, all national publications. The magazines *Apsi, Cauce, Análisis*, and *Hoy*, the newspapers *La Epoca* and *Fortín Mapocho*, provide the opposition with an impressive communications capability. Even though the government has banned access to television, a number of national and provincial radio stations are open to the opposition and will broadcast its messages. It is a pity that these messages are so often confused.

The opposition politicians must find younger leaders to replace the traditional party bosses. They must also learn to be humbler in their approach to reality. It would undoubtedly do them good to digest what they were told in April 1987 by Patricio Aylwin, former president of the Christian Democratic Party* and one of its historic figures: "When I was twenty and my generation was twenty, there were many injustices in this

---

*Aylwin became party president again several months later.

country and much inequality, but there was freedom. We were proud of Chilean democracy. The men of that era proposed—some within the framework of social Christian ideas, others in the framework of Socialist ideas, and others more radical—to end the injustices and transform this country, constructing a new Chile that would be just, humane, and with solidarity, while conserving freedom. Fifty years later there is more injustice and we do not have freedom. We are a failed generation."

In his frank reading of the Chilean situation, Aylwin said more: "The Chileans do not know how to fight under a dictatorship. It is not clear that we have learned. There are reasons to be disillusioned about the country in general. We have always believed that Chileans were courageous, but the vast majority are fairly cowardly."

Something else enriched affairs in Chile in April 1987, following John Paul's visit: The pope entrusted to the Catholic Church the task of bringing reconciliation to Chile. A journalist wrote in *Apsi* that Chile went on being Chile, despite the pope. In truth, it could not have been otherwise. Yet by maintaining its strength in the struggle for human rights, the Church has begun to develop a new strategy that complements the priority of reconciliation that the pope has urged. Reconciliation may be expressed in spiritual terms, but the opposition can insist on political answers. The opposition now has a new instrument in the peaceful struggle for democracy. Reconciliation, as the Church understands it, calls upon both sides to move closer without concern for the distance between them. Who gives what will not be for the Church to decide. It will depend on the strength of Pinochet and that of the opposition and also on the intelligence of both.

Of course, only a united Church could carry out this task, so reconciliation must begin from within. The first results have been a strengthening of the moderate bishops who have been joined by the progressive priests. The divisions that have so often helped Pinochet in the past and will probably help him if he remains in power will, in this instance at least, be contained within a theological framework. The pope would have aggravated the divisions within the Church if he had confronted Pinochet directly and publicly. Paris may be worth a mass, but Pinochet is not worth a schism.

Reconciliation has its ludicrous aspects as well. José Zabala, president of the Social Union of Christian Businessmen, and unofficial adviser to the primate of the Catholic Church, believes that thanks to the pope there are signs of reconciliation outside politics: "I have seen them and I am encouraged by them. Among various cases is that of my friend, a lawyer, who had begun a huge lawsuit, over an inheritance, against his brother. After the pope left, they reached an agreement not to go ahead with the matter."

Reconciliation, of course, also has its controversial side, stemming from each party's failure to understand the limits to what the other is prepared to concede. When a government functionary announced that reconciliation "is possible only within the framework of the present institutional system," the opposition replied that this "is the equivalent of a demand for an unconditional surrender of the civilian sector to the political agenda that the military regime seeks to impose and which it assumes will perpetuate it in power."

The danger for the democratic opposition is that once again, as has happened so often in the 1980s, the government has demonstrated greater initiative. Pinochet reacted swiftly to make himself the first to respond to the idea of reconciliation. He presented to Archbishop Juan Francisco Fresno the gold medal that he should have given him two years before, when he was made cardinal by the pope. Cardinal Fresno, who provides fundamental support for the Vicarage of Solidarity, accepted the decoration and attended the ceremony that the government organized for the occasion. A few days later, the regime canceled its authorization for the CNI, the state intelligence service, to arrest politicians and also its right to maintain detention centers, those shocking clandestine prisons that were truly Nazi concentration camps in miniature.

There is another aspect of Chilean reality that may be easier to understand when viewed in the light of the Spanish experience. During the final fifteen years of Franco's rule the right wing formed part of the government and controlled the political, juridical, economic, and cultural institutions. At the same time the right developed an understanding of the future similar to that of Felipe González and, in an antidemocratic context, developed a democratic personality. The opportunity of the Right came when it guided the Spanish polity toward a full transition to democracy, without prejudice to the opposition though also without apparent remorse for its own past links to the terrible fascist dictatorship. It opened the doors to political participation for all elements of the spectrum, from left to right, and tolerated the explosion of all the nationalistic and regional aspirations, political and cultural, that it had helped suppress for many years. No less important was the fact that this increased participation did not take a violent or uncontrolled course—the only demands made were oriented toward the future, and did not overstep the bounds of the possible. And if the political right deserved credit for accepting the inevitability of change in society, the democratic opposition, for its part, did not claim to find in this inevitability any right to act like a conqueror in enemy territory.

In Chile, in April 1987, one could discern an expansion of the territory held by the democratic opposition, in the emergence of a right wing that, without renouncing the present regime, recognizes its exhaustion. This new right does not repent of its past struggle against the democratic opposition—indeed, hopes to continue the struggle—but acknowledges that it must now be conducted on new terrain. Fixing the boundaries of this terrain, that is to say, negotiating the transition, is now the principal demand upon the political intelligence of both the right and the opposition. It is a field of which the Church can project an image in spiritual terms, but it is the politicians who must plow and sow it, and reap the harvest from it.

Apart from nationality, two things separate Felipe González and Andrés Allamand. The Chilean is shorter and he is politically on the right. But the call for the acceptance of reality that Felipe González made in Suresnes in 1974 is what fires Andrés Allamand today. The Chilean has a face that is youthful and fresh. His smile is welcoming, his laughter is expressive. And he is convinced that the only political intelligence that can open the door to democracy in Chile is that of the right.

In his office in the center of Santiago, a few hundred yards from Government House, all the words he has pronounced or written are neatly printed and filed. He is forthright in his opinions and he does not indulge the Chilean tendency for subtlety or romantic interpretation. Although it is hard to say whether he is rigid or extremely determined, it is even more difficult to deny his political vocation just because he is inclined to make predictions rather than analyses.

In April 1987 he revealed the role that the right wing is prepared to play in the political arena when he referred to the matter touchiest for the military—the possibility of trials for the murders and torture carried out since 1973. In conversations with the armed forces Allamand said he had proposed: "Resolve the existing problems relating to human rights by an equation that will balance vengeance and impunity."

The unknown question that remains, in any case, is whether a right wing that believes in elections more open than those proposed by the dictatorship and whose mistrust of the government is awakening—it criticizes the regime as caustically as it does the opposition—can put the transition into gear. Allamand said in April 1987, "I believe that they have both been mistaken, the opposition because it has maintained its central demand: the fall of the government; and the government because it has demanded unconditional surrender of the opposition. An understanding calls for the parties to meet each other halfway. The first thing that has to be understood by both is that there is not going to be any unconditional surrender by either of the two sides. There is a process, and that process must be carried out within the existing institutional order, and all the possibilities that open up must be utilized so that this imperfect transition culminates in the best way possible."

The right may need to give more to Chile if it is to make the transition work. It must renounce the pillaging of the Chilean economy, a privilege it has exercised to the full and that has plunged large sectors of the population into misery. If it had not been for the terror unleashed against them, these sectors would not have allowed themselves to be deprived of the barest necessities of life. Even when the Church, with its enormous prestige, helps console victims of repression, this consolation is of no use to those who are desperately in need of food, housing and employment.

The right wing believes it is more realistic than the present regime and the opposition. Every time the right makes a pronouncement it calls upon the government and the opposition to abandon the realm of fantasy. The right wing must also accept that it, too, must abstain from such childishness—even though escape into fantasy may be politically astute.

TESTIMONY

My name is Jacobo Timerman. I am visiting Chile after an absence of fifteen years, and from my window in the Hotel Carrera I have a clear view of the Palacio de la Moneda, which is barely 100 yards away. The Carrera and Government House face each other across the Plaza de la Constitución. There are no trees or monuments between them to obstruct the view.

The last two people I saw before I left back then both died in La Moneda, on September 11, 1973, the day of the military coup. They were President Salvador Allende and my friend the journalist Augusto Olivares.

I remember days of intense conversation with Olivares and two long interviews with Allende, one in Viña del Mar and the other at the presidential residence. As I have thought about them so many times during this present visit, the temptation to indulge in nostalgia is much stronger than the will to confront the dramatic reality that I must face.

I remember Augusto Olivares, his spectacles with their thick lenses, his robust physique, his luxuriant mustache. For many years he was the most popular figure among the journalists who used to cover the conferences of the Organization of American States. He had that special charm, that appeal that the Chileans call *angel*. He liked to invent songs, and sometimes Juan de Onís, the *New York Times* correspondent, would accompany him on the guitar while Irmano Alves of the *Jornal do Brasil* would tap out the beat with a spoon on the wine glasses. Sometimes we would make a little mischief together. Once, in Montevideo in 1961, during an impromptu birthday party, we got Comandante Ernesto Ché Guevara together with White House adviser Richard Goodwin. It wasn't easy for President Kennedy's adviser on Latin America to explain that conversation, alone, with a guerrilla leader, when he returned to Washington. At the time we fantasized about the importance of that dialogue in 1961. We were proved wrong. It accomplished nothing.

I remember Augusto Olivares too in Punta del Este in 1962, when Cuba was expelled from the Organization of American States. The early risers among the journalists covering the conference could find us drinking beer with correspondent Tad Szulc, who was practicing his precariously grasped Serbian with colleagues from the newspaper *Politika* and the Tanjug news agency. In the evening we would meet again to exchange information with the ubiquitous Ted Cordova Claure.

The memories came flooding in one gray day in Santiago toward the end of 1986. I realized that we were all alive, except Augusto Olivares. We had all had our experiences. Ted Cordova Claure was taken out of his country, Bolivia, in an ambulance plane, with several bullets in his body, after a military coup, and since then the one constant in his life has been exile. Irmano Alves was also exiled for many years during the Brazilian military dictatorship. And I was kidnapped, imprisoned, tortured, and exiled. We are alive, but Olivares is dead.

I remember a morning in Viña del Mar. I was walking with Augusto Olivares and the director Costa-Gavras while he was making *State of Siege*, a film about the military repression in Uruguay. We never imagined that a few years later he would make *Missing* about the Chilean drama. We didn't imagine that, but we must have had some presentiment, because Chile was gripped by a strange unreality, as if something was about to happen. Olivares was worried about the pressure the extreme left was exerting on President Allende, which was preventing him from formulating a coherent strategy. The left was making impossible demands, almost as if it was out to destabilize the government. Olivares told me about the activities of the CIA, about the conspiracies of the U.S. Embassy and the irresponsibility of top Chilean financiers, and of the coup-mongering of the Edwards family, the owners of *El Mercurio*.

During the interview with Salvador Allende in his residence in Santiago, the same themes kept coming up. The president was a lively and agreeable conversationalist. He was refined and witty, proud to offer me the cheese the Dutch ambassador had given him, but even prouder of the high quality of the Chilean wines that were on the table.

We were interrupted by a visit from Carlos Altamirano, an intellectualized aristocrat, the leader of the extreme left. Altamirano was demanding, at that critical time, that the country be organized as a popular republic and that the right-wing offensive be countered by arming popular militias. After he left, Allende commented that Altamirano had not digested all the romanticism associated with the Sierra Maestra. He did not hide his disgust at the attitude of this elegant leftist, though that did not change the agreeable tone of the conversation. At the time the leader of the Communist Party, Luis Corvalán, responded with an extremely sharp criticism of the suicidal infantilism of Altamirano. A pamphlet with Corvalán's reply to Altamirano's proposals was widely circulated. It seemed to me that his was a voice of prudence and reason in the midst of the confusion of the extreme left and the subversive violence of the right.

Salvador Allende impressed me as a magnificent political leader, an enchanting person, and a dedicated reader, but he did not have the stature of a statesman. He enjoyed politics, but did not seem comfortable running the government. It looked to me—or, at least, I had the feeling—that he was a little lost in the pandemonium that was Chile a year before he was overthrown.

There in La Moneda, facing the window of my room in the Carrera, they both died. I have been told many times of their death. Costa-Gavras described it to me when he visited my home in Tel Aviv and again when I saw him in Paris. Yet, even as I look at the reconstructed La Moneda, fifteen years afterward, it is hard for me to believe that Augusto Olivares, that magnificent Latin American, is no more.

That's how Chile is. A truncated country, with missing elements that seem unacceptable, unthinkable. For me, forever, Chile will be the country without Augusto. I also discovered, when I went to Isla Negra, that I will have to learn to accept that it is the country without Pablo Neruda. My Chile no longer exists.

My wife, Risha, arrived from Buenos Aires to stay for three days, in November 1986, to join me on a pilgrimage to Neruda's houses in Isla Negra, in Valparaíso, and in Santiago. The common destiny of lovers in Latin America is to return again and again to Pablo Neruda. He accompanied us from our first kisses; he helped us to get through, with sensuality, our early adolescence; he was with us during our first major political upheaval—the civil war, the fall of the Spanish Republic, and the fascist inferno that followed. With Neruda we were able to grasp and understand the earthy romance and magic of Latin America and we also walked with him over the bridge he laid down to the United States when he sang to Abraham Lincoln, "May the woodcutter awake," with no less pain and passion than Walt Whitman. Not even the bad poems imbued with his loyalty to communism or his homage to Stalin could diminish in any way the presence of Neruda in our dreams and our romances. No particle of our sensibility could be separated from the poet. His words and his rhythms will forever be the only expression that we Latin Americans have when our heart overflows with love for another human or with love of the universe.

Neruda called it Isla Negra, "Black Island," although it is not an island. It is an elbow of land with a tiny bridge to cross a minute inlet of the sea. But he loved islands, seas, boats, and ports. Some eighty-five miles from Santiago, on the Pacific Ocean, he built his house on a pile of rocks on which pilgrims like Risha and me write, paint, curse, threaten, and remember. The house on Isla Negra is, in fact, a number of houses. Neruda added houses as he dreamed them up. The place is now silent, surrounded by a high wall that seals it off. The wall is formed by canes laced together. The pilgrims circle round the wall, peering from time to time through the cracks. A shadow may fall on the house, a dog may bark. A dirt track runs by the side of the house to the sea, and on a sunny day we can lie on the same small sandy beach where Neruda warmed himself.

With great difficulty I secured permission to enter the garden. The house is closed and its door sealed with strips of paper bearing the stamp of a judge of the regime. The poet had left the house to the Communist Party and the government confiscated all the party's assets. The Pablo Neruda Foundation is trying to recover the house to make it into a museum, as is happening to his home in Santiago.

The sadness that descended upon us made conversation impossible. Even when we recited his poetry, it did not help. One wants to come in contact with the living Neruda, or to enter his life in some way; but the objects spread around the garden, like the old harvester that looks like a locomotive and that he loved so much, are not consoling. He died of cancer on September 23, 1973, twelve days after the coup. He knew what was happening.

Chile is an unusual country. It has only two Nobel Prize winners, both of them poets: Gabriela Mistral and Pablo Neruda.

Risha and I went to Valparaíso, where we looked for, but did not find, the house that he called La Sebastiana, and then on to Santiago, where we visited La Chascona, now in the midst of reconstruction. Our three days were Nerudian days, melancholy, but with the heart calm as Neruda liked. We shielded ourselves as much as possible from reality so as not to lose, perhaps, the last Nerudism, knowing that when Risha went back to Buenos Aires, I would return to the disappeared, the murdered, the widows, the orphans, the political confusion, and the general exhaustion.

A Chilean, Irene Geis, was my secretary at my newspaper *La Opinión* when I was kidnapped by the Argentine military. Her German passport allowed her to escape to Europe. Some years later she managed to return to Chile. There wasn't much point in questioning her, asking her why she had decided to face the risks that living in Chile implied. I have put this question to many exiles, and I now know that Chileans cannot live outside Chile, or they don't know how. Through Irene I met Carmen Hertz.

I really wasn't prepared for this encounter. The three of us lunched in a fashionable restaurant, observing the Chilean ritual of shellfish, fish, and wine. Carmen Hertz was an elegant, delicate woman, aged about thirty-five, with heavy black wavy hair and a white face with a sharp, clearly defined profile. Only the eyes, matched by high cheekbones, were in accord with her spirit, because, like her, they were always combative and there was no way of making them quiet down. Even now, as I write and look at photographs of her, I can carry on a discussion with the eyes of Carmen Hertz.

I was not prepared, because at no moment did we depart from the topics that are of such passionate interest to people interested in politics. Additionally, despite the gap between our generations, we had interests in common—books, art, and music. Irene Geis and I are spontaneous without any system. Carmen is spontaneous and laughs uproariously, but her lawyer's mind opens like a flower in debate and she doesn't give way.

Carmen Hertz's husband disappeared on October 19, 1973, and his body was never found. Although I have conducted dozens of interviews with wives, children, and mothers of people who have been detained and have disappeared, I was not prepared when I realized at the end of our lively conversation that she was the wife of someone who had disappeared. Purely and simply, the wife of a disappeared person.

The drama of a disappearance is of such magnitude that in general the conversation with a relative rarely gets beyond the interminable enumeration of details, dates, and dashed hopes. There is no way to assimilate so much tragedy. Carmen Hertz does not exhibit that incomprehension of the universe, that withdrawal and separation from the rest of the world, which I have observed in other relatives of disappeared people. Carmen is a lawyer at the Vicariate of Solidarity who must listen to relatives repeat again and again what she knows from her own experience. Shortly after the coup that killed Allende, Carlos Berger Guralnik, Carmen's husband, was tried by a Council of War and condemned to sixty-one days in prison. He ran a radio station in the mining zone of Chuquicamata. Carmen took clean clothes, food, and a little consolation to the jail. October 19, 1973, was no different from any other visiting day at the jail. Only two weeks remained for the completion of his sentence, and they talked about his release, about the journey they would make to Santiago, about their baby. At five o'clock that afternoon Carmen said goodbye to her husband. At six o'clock, Carlos was handcuffed, blindfolded, and taken from the jail in an army truck. He was shot in an unknown place, and his body was never recovered. He was one of the victims of Calama.

The relatives of disappeared people usually tell these stories. Carmen doesn't. She raised her son, who is now a teenager. She commenced lawsuits against functionaries and military officers in the courts. She has behaved like a lawyer and a wife. She asked for Carlos's body. She asked for justice. Finally, she managed to identify the man responsible for the shooting of her husband, General Sergio Arellano Stark. She has brought criminal charges against this officer, who directed the firing squads in north and central Chile.

Carmen Hertz speaks of other things. She talks about her global idea of how justice should be in Chile before she mentions her own personal tragedy. You have to divine for yourself, amid a torrent of political convictions and juridical proposals, her intimate pain.

We met one night in Irene Geis's house, in an enchanting neighborhood of small homes surrounded by gardens. Knowing that her husband's presumptive murderer is no longer anonymous, she feels calmer. But her emphasis remains on the same themes: the cowardice of the military who murder people after handcuffing them and covering their heads with hoods, and then hide their bodies. She also insists that Chilean society can be reconstituted morally only if there is a collective act of conscience over the horror of these years. "When I say that it must be collective, I mean that each and every one of the violations of human rights must be known by each and every one in Chile," she said.

I think it would be a symbol for all Latin America if Carmen Hertz manages to put General Sergio Arellano Stark in a prison cell. While she is trying to do just that, Carmen brings up a son who knows about his father only from newspaper stories and a few photographs. It is a typical situation in Chile, and elsewhere in Latin America.

It is difficult to evade certain topics in Chile, and the disappeared constitute one of them. I have attempted to console Chileans by telling them that in Argentina it was much more terrible. In Argentina, some twenty thousand vanished out of a population of 32 million; in Chile, there are seven hundred missing out of 11 million. But the pain caused by the wound of a disappearance cannot be measured in numbers.

Just the same, you can sit with someone in the Bellavista quarter of Santiago and you can remain silent, or you can sing if you feel like it. In the Café del Cerro there is a dance school, a theater workshop, and an exhibition of paintings. It is a typical Spanish-style building with a large central patio and a rickety staircase that leads to the upper floor. I am in the patio with Joan Jara, the English ballerina who returned to Chile after ten years in exile. Before she left Chile with her two small daughters, under the protection of the British consul, she had to search among hundreds of anonymous corpses for the body of her husband, Victor Jara, who was murdered in the National Stadium, where Pinochet's first concentration camp functioned. She took his body and placed it in a niche in the General Cemetery in Santiago.

She had agreed to see me for an interview because I too had been a political prisoner of the military. She recalled that I was the first to publish what had happened to Victor Jara. She doesn't give interviews anymore. We spoke less about the past and more about her work as director of the dance school in the Café del Cerro. She gives free classes to poor students and produces shows for the people of the marginal settlements. She gave me a copy of the book she has written about the life of Victor Jara, *An Unfinished Song*, and she underlined the first paragraph of the preface for me: "It is a relief, at last, to tell this story quietly, in my own way, instead of responding to sudden questions which allow me to tell only the parts of it which interest the person who is interviewing me."

I was not interviewing her, so our silences were not uncomfortable. She is quite at home here. One of her daughters came up to greet me. She had that extraordinary serenity that I have noted in other children whose parents have been murdered by the military. They are like missionaries who have a hope that cannot be shaken. Joan returned to Chile because her identity is there and because of her loyalty to what Victor Jara signifies in this tormented country. Identity and loyalty, those beautiful examples of human architecture that the military dictatorships would like to demolish. Joan Jara is a complete, warmhearted woman. She does her work, she dances. And she waits.

Questions of identity and loyalty were, for several years, the drama of Juan Pablo Letelier, who assisted me during my visit to Chile. In his home I got to know other young Chileans. I went with him to the theater, to meetings with journalists, writers, lawyers, politicians, and priests. He was restrained and reserved and his spiritual identity was for me a very gradual discovery. I had known his father, Orlando Letelier, when he was Allende's foreign minister. I met his mother, Isabel Letelier, years later in Washington, after I had been released from prison.

Juan Pablo is twenty-six. He was twelve when Orlando Letelier was arrested in Santiago, after the coup. He was fifteen when his father was killed in Washington. He was twenty-two when he decided to return to a country he hardly knew and whose language he spoke with difficulty. He had been born and educated in the United States. He had traveled around the world, but everything seemed distant and strange. His mind was fixed on the father who had been taken away from him and whose enormous presence in the family had been removed. Only recently, one day in Germany, young and desperate, did he manage to cry. It was then that he worked out his identity as a Chilean and as the son of Orlando Letelier, and also his loyalty to the father who was assassinated in Washington by a bomb from Pinochet. He tells it like this: "I remember that one day during Easter, on that journey, I could cry. I was in a woods in Germany, in a children's playground covered with snow. I cried there for hours—for myself, for my family, which I love so much. I felt all the weight of my loneliness."

One night, when part of Santiago was dark because of a power outage, I was in Juan Pablo's home and we had dinner by the candles that surrounded the table. It was inevitable that we should comment on the fact that there had been a new upsurge of repression. But Juan Pablo was optimistic. He was proud of the modest home he had put together with his wife. He has a spontaneous laugh, like his mother, and he talks carefully, rationally, as I had heard his father talk in 1973 in the Chilean Embassy in Buenos Aires. Every September 21, the day they murdered Orlando Letelier, he walks alone through the streets of Santiago. Before, he went walking on that day to think over the things he had been discussing as an adolescent with his father and which had been interrupted. Now it is different: "I want him to tell me if I am doing well or badly. I think I want him to be proud of me."

When the new magazine *Pluma y Pincel* was launched at the Book Fair in Santiago, a large group of writers and journalists got together. We celebrated the birth of the new magazine, and then we went to La Candela in the Bellavista quarter, to eat empanadas and drink warm wine. And we also went to sing—and did we sing!—the songs of Violeta Parra and Victor Jara.

The two folklore singers, Charo Cofré and Hugo Arévalo, who formed an act together, returned from exile in Europe after ten years, and they are on stage at La Candela almost every night. When they fled from Chile, they stayed in my home in Buenos Aires, and some other Chileans stayed in my brother's home. Later they all left for Europe, and I had not seen them since. There cannot be anything more joyous than to be reunited with old Chilean friends, to sing and to drink warm wine until dawn. It was the weekend, and the curfew had been lifted.

I thought to myself at one moment during the long night that the parable that began with Augusto Olivares was ending in the best possible way, with this reencounter. But my friendship with Olivares was of another dimension. Nevertheless, there we were in Chile, in Santiago, singing the prohibited songs, amidst the tree-lined streets of Bellavista, with the big old windows of La Candela opened wide. It is true we were singing with a certain apprehension, perhaps even a touch of fear; but we were singing.

A week later, *Pluma y Pincel* was banned by General Augusto Pinochet. The editors had to wait for three months and take advantage of the relaxation of censorship prompted by the visit of the pope before they could publish the second issue.

Before I completed this book, I telephoned Santiago. They told me that yes, they still sing in Bellavista and drink warm wine in La Candela. Undoubtedly one does feel better knowing this is so.

Buenos Aires, April 1987

ABOUT THE AUTHOR

JACOBO TIMERMAN was born in the Ukrainian town of Bar in 1923, and moved with his family to Argentina in 1928. A lifelong journalist, he founded two weekly newsmagazines in the 1960s and was a prominent news commentator on radio and television. He was the editor and publisher of the newspaper *La Opinion* from 1971 until his arrest by military authorities on April 15, 1977. Released in September 1979, he lived in Tel Aviv, Madrid, and New York. He is the author of *Prisoner Without a Name, Cell Without a Number* and *The Longest War,* which are also available from Vintage. Mr. Timerman returned in 1984 to Buenos Aires, where he lives now.